Flux Theatre in association v
the Finborough Theatre pre:

The world premiere

Dubailand

by Carmen Nasr

FINBOROUGH | THEATRE

First performed at the Finborough Theatre as a staged reading as part of *Vibrant 2015 – A Festival of Finborough Playwrights.* Sunday, 25 October 2015.

First performance at the Finborough Theatre: Sunday, 5 February 2017.

Dubailand

By Carmen Nasr

Cast in order of speaking

Amar	**Adi Chugh**
Clara	**Mitzli Rose Neville**
Tanveer	**Varun Sharma**
Tommie	**Leon Williams**
Amanda	**Belinda Stewart-Wilson**
Deena	**Reena Lalbihari**
Jamie	**Nicholas Banks**
Lali	**Aanya Chadha**

The action takes place in Dubai, present day.

The performance lasts approximately ninety minutes.

There will be no interval.

Director	**Georgie Staight**
Designer	**Bex Kemp**
Lighting Designer	**Robbie Butler**
Sound Designer	**Jack Burton**
Stage Manager / Assistant Director	**Wiebke Green**
Producer	**Caley Powell**

Our patrons are respectfully reminded that, in this intimate theatre, any noise such as rustling programmes, talking or the ringing of mobile phones may distract the actors and your fellow audience members.

We regret there is no admittance or re-admittance to the auditorium whilst the performance is in progress.

Dubailand is performed in repertoire and on the set of *Run The Beast Down* which plays Tuesday to Saturday evenings, and Saturday and Sunday matinees, until 25 February 2017.

Nicholas Banks | Jamie
Trained at Guildhall School of Music and Drama.
Theatre includes *The Shawshank Redemption*
(National Tour), *Punk Rock* (Royal Exchange
Theatre, Manchester, Lyric Theatre,
Hammersmith, and National Tour), *People Like
Us* (Pleasance London), *The Happiest Day of
Your Life* (Vineyard Theatre, New York) and *24
Hour Plays* (Old Vic 24 Hour Plays at The Old
Vic).
Film includes *Kingsman: The Secret Service,
Synced* and *Seat 25*.
Television includes *Law and Order* and
Pramface.

Aanya Chadha | Lali
Currently attends Future Stars Stage School and
has been involved in a number of productions
whilst training.

Adi Chugh | Amar
Trained at Bristol Old Vic Theatre School and
short courses at London Academy of Music
and Dramatic Art, New York City Acting
School for Film and Television, Pennsylvania
State University, with New Delhi's The Ilhaam
Collective and Third Bell Theatre Company, New
Delhi.
Theatre includes *5 Guys Chillin'* (SoHo
Playhouse, New York, King's Head Theatre
and Edinburgh Festival), *Northanger Abbey*
(Wickham Theatre, Bristol), *Frankenstein* (John
Wesley Chapel, Bristol), *27 Wagons Full of
Cotton* (Wits Theatre Complex, Johannesburg),
Ashadh Ka Ek Din (One Day Before The Rainy
Season) (Actor Factor Theatre Company, New
Delhi) and *Apne Fan Ka Ustad* (The Master
of His Art) (Third Bell Theatre Company, New
Delhi).
Film includes *3 Dots and A Dash* and *Pool
Sharks*.

Reena Lalbihari | Deena
Trained at East 15 Acting School.
Theatre includes *Faustus* (Headlong Theatre), *Madame du Sade* (Donmar Warehouse), *Pole Factor* (VAULT Festival) and *Londonee* (Mukul and Ghetto Tigers Theatre Company).
Film includes *Temptation, Halal Harry, Final Score* and *The Children Act.*
Television includes *EastEnders, MIHigh, Day of the Triffids* and *The Bill.* Web series includes *Tempting Fates.*

Miztli Rose Neville | Clara
Productions at the Finborough Theatre include *The Great Divide.*
Trained at the Royal Academy of Dramatic Art.
Theatre includes *Christmas at Mildred's* (Hen and Chickens Theatre), *How The Vote Was Won* and *Pot Kettle* (Bloomsbury Festival) and *The Pursuit of App-iness* and *Birdwatching* (Gielgud Theatre).
Film includes *Crown for Christmas.*
Radio includes *Ballerina Feet.* Miztli is a co-host of the podcast *Heroine Addicts.*

Varun Sharma | Tanveer (and multiple roles)
Trained at Mountview Academy of Theatre Arts.
Theatre includes *Billy and Girl* (Karamel Club) and *In Soft Wings* (Tristan Bates Theatre).
Film includes *Baar Baar Dekho* (See It Again).
Television includes *Hear Of The Year Promo* and *Lenovo K5 Note.*

Belinda Stewart-Wilson | Amanda
Trained at Webber Douglas Academy.
Theatre includes *The Kitchen* (Royal Court Theatre), *United Biscuits Double Act* (Canal Café Theatre) and *Shady Business* (The Mill at Sonning).
Film includes *The Brother, Inbetweeners 2* (The Long Goodbye), *All That Way for Love, The Inbetweeners, Huge, Kiss Kiss (Bang Bang),*

Razzle Dazzle (*A Journey into Dance*), *La Passione* and *Move*.
Television includes *Sick Note, The Inbetweeners, Hetty Feather, Evermoor, Ordinary Lies, Ripper Street, Citizen Khan, Mr Sloane, Little Crackers, Holy Flying Circus, Popatron, Miranda, The Morgana Show, New Tricks, Whites, Primeval, The Peter Serafinowicz Show* and *The IT Crowd*.

Leon Williams | Tommie
Trained at Guildhall School of Music and Drama. Theatre includes *One Man, Two Guvnors* (National Tour), *Hobson's Choice, Romeo and Juliet* and *Twelfth Night* (Open Air Theatre, Regent's Park), *A Midsummer Night's Dream* and *King James Bible* (Shakespeare's Globe), *Great Expectations* (Library Theatre, Manchester), *Skylight* (Stephen Joseph Theatre, Scarborough), *Wink* (Theatre503), *Lesere* (Jermyn Street Theatre), *Crimes Of The Heart* (Union Theatre), *A Midsummer Night's Dream* (Peter Hall Company), *As You Like It* (Rose Theatre, Kingston), *The Bullet* (Royal Shakespeare Company at Hampstead Theatre), *Private Peaceful* (National tour), *Not About Heroes* (Royal Lyceum Theatre, Edinburgh), *The Changeling* (English Touring Theatre), *As You Like It* (Derby Playhouse), *Charley's Aunt* (Oxford Playhouse) and *An Ideal Husband* (Chichester Festival Theatre).
Film includes *Toilets* and *Sceptre*.
Television includes *New Tricks, Call The Midwife* and *Ford and Abram*.
Leon also narrates various audiobooks and voices several animation characters.

Carmen Nasr | Playwright
Carmen is a British-Lebanese playwright, and is currently Channel 4 Playwrights Scheme Playwright in Residence at the Finborough Theatre, supported by the Peggy Ramsay Foundation. *Dubailand* received a staged reading at *Vibrant 2015 – A Festival of Finborough Playwrights*. Her first play *The House of My Father* received a staged reading at *Vibrant 2014 – A Festival of Finborough Playwrights* and was also part of the annual Nour Festival of Contemporary Middle Eastern and North African Art and Culture. In 2015, *The House of My Father* was longlisted for the Bruntwood Prize, and in 2015 she was shortlisted for the OffWestEnd Adopt a Playwright Award.

Georgie Staight | Director
Trained at Mountview Academy of Theatre Arts. Theatre includes *Dreamless Sleep* (Arts Theatre), *Bridle* (Tristan Bates Theatre), *Doomed Resistance* (Arcola Theatre) and *Next of Kin* (Bristol Old Vic). She is currently Joint Artistic Director of Flux Theatre.
She is also a playwright and has directed her own work, including the adaptation and world premiere of Deborah Levy's *Billy and Girl* (Karamel Club), *Let There Be Light* (Chichester Festival Theatre) and *Blue Moon* (Clifton Theatre, Bristol).

Bex Kemp | Set and Costume Designer
Productions at the Finborough Theatre include *Andy Capp The Musical*.
Trained at Royal Central School of Speech and Drama where she designed *Pentecost, Variations of the Death of Trotsky, Scenes From The Big Picture* and *The Common Chorus*.
Designs include *Othello* (Greenwich Theatre and National tour), *Becoming Mohammed* (Pleasance London and The Space), *About Miss Julie* (King's Head Theatre), *Circling the Square* (Salisbury Arts Centre), *As You Like It* (National Tour) and *Our Space* (LOST Theatre).
Costume designs include: *F*ck the Polar Bears* (Bush Theatre). Design Assistant work includes *Iphigenia Quartet* (Gate Theatre), *The Boy Who Climbed Out Of His Face* (Shunt) and *The Duchess of Malfi* (Punchdrunk). She has also worked as assistant to Miriam Buether. Costume design for film include: *All of Me*.

Robbie Butler | Lighting Designer
Productions at the Finborough Theatre include *Run The Beast Down* and *Don't Smoke In Bed*.
Trained at the Royal Conservatoire of Scotland. He was the winner of the 2015 ETC Award from the Association of Lighting Designers and was nominated for an OffWestEnd Award for Best Lighting Design for his work on *Odd Shaped Balls* (Old Red Lion Theatre).
Lighting designs include *Scapegoat* (St Stephen's Church), *Poppies: A New Musical* (The Space) and *The Merchant of Venice* (Kaohsiung Spring Arts Festival, Taiwan).
Technician work includes *No's Knife, Groundhog Day* and *Dr Seuss's The Lorax* (The Old Vic) and *Cirque Du Soleil's Amaluna* (Touring Big Top).
www.robbiebutlerdesigns.com

Jack Barton | Sound Designer
Trained at the University of Manchester, receiving the P.J. Leonard Prize for Electroacoustic Composition.
Sound designs include *You/Me/Tomorrow* (HOME, Manchester), *The Tempest* (Chelsea Theatre and Etcetera Theatre), *Pizza Delique* (Edinburgh Festival), *Sharp Edges* (Lion and Unicorn Theatre, Etcetera Theatre and Camden People's Theatre), *The Porcelain Girl* (Hive Mind), and *Breathing Corpses, Animal Farm* and *Pit* (University of Manchester).
Sound Designer and composition for film includes: *Tabula Rasa, Tape* and *Elevator Blues*.
Composition includes performances of new work at the Royal Welsh College of Music and Drama, the Anthony Burgess Foundation and in collaboration with Manchester Theatre in Sound.
Jack received a nomination for Best Sound Designer from the London OffWestEnd Awards 2016 for *The Tempest* (Etcetera Theatre) and was awarded Best Sound Design in 2015 by the Manchester In Fringe Theatre Awards.
jackbarton.wordpress.com

Wiebke Green | Stage Manager / Assistant Director
Theatre includes Assistant Production and Stage Management on *The Frontier Trilogy* and *Sirenia* (Edinburgh Festival) and Stage Management on *Housed* (Old Vic New Voices).

Caley Powell | Producer

Theatre includes *Wendy House* (VAULT Festival), *Othello* and *Twelfth Night* (Upstairs at the Gatehouse), *Never The Same* (Bridewell Theatre) and *Might Never Happen* (King's Head Theatre).

Co-producing includes *Never Ending Night* (The Vaults).

She has also worked as Assistant Producer on *East End Boys and West End Girls* (Courtyard Theatre) and *Loaded* (Brockley Jack Studio Theatre) and as Production Assistant on *Nutcracker: The Musical* (Pleasance London) and *Palindrome Productions Summer Season* (Courtyard Theatre).

Caley also works as a Casting director, runs the production company Flitter Films and produces *The Deleted Scene Podcast*.

Production Acknowledgements

Dubailand has been funded through kind donations made as part of *Dubailand's* Crowdfunding campaign. Thank you to Press Representative Susie Safavi and Casting Director Aurora Causin.

FINBOROUGH | THEATRE
VIBRANT **NEW WRITING** | UNIQUE **REDISCOVERIES**

"Probably the most influential fringe theatre in the world."
Time Out

"No small theatre in Britain has a larger impact on the theatrical ecology than the tiny Finborough in Earl's Court... Even the National and Royal Court are hard pressed to make as many discoveries (or rediscoveries) as it routinely does"
Mark Shenton, The Stage – Top Venues 2016

"The tiny but mighty Finborough...one of the best batting averages of any London company" Ben Brantley, The New York Times

Founded in 1980, the multi-award-winning Finborough Theatre presents plays and music theatre, concentrated exclusively on vibrant new writing and unique rediscoveries from the 19th and 20th centuries. Our programme is unique – never presenting work that has been seen anywhere in London during the last 25 years. Behind the scenes, we continue to discover and develop a new generation of theatre makers – most notably through our annual festival of new writing – *Vibrant – A Festival of Finborough Playwrights*.

Despite remaining completely unsubsidised, the Finborough Theatre has an unparalleled track record of attracting the finest talent who go on to become leading voices in British theatre. Under Artistic Director Neil McPherson, it has discovered some of the UK's most exciting new playwrights including Laura Wade, James Graham, Mike Bartlett, Jack Thorne, Simon Vinnicombe, Alexandra Wood, Nicholas de Jongh and Anders Lustgarten; and directors including Blanche McIntyre, Robert Hastie and Sam Yates.

Artists working at the theatre in the 1980s included Clive Barker, Rory Bremner, Nica Burns, Kathy Burke, Ken Campbell, Jane Horrocks and Claire Dowie. In the 1990s, the Finborough Theatre first became known for new writing including Naomi Wallace's first play *The War Boys*; Rachel Weisz in David Farr's *Neville Southall's Washbag*; four plays by Anthony Neilson including *Penetrator* and *The Censor*, both of which transferred to the Royal Court Theatre; and new plays by Richard Bean, Lucinda Coxon, David Eldridge, Tony Marchant and Mark Ravenhill. New writing development included the premieres of modern classics such as Mark Ravenhill's *Shopping and F***king*, Conor McPherson's *This Lime Tree Bower*; Naomi Wallace's *Slaughter City* and Martin McDonagh's *The Pillowman*.

Since 2000, new British plays have included Laura Wade's London debut *Young Emma*, commissioned for the Finborough Theatre; two one-woman shows by Miranda Hart; James Graham's *Albert's Boy* with Victor Spinetti; Sarah Grochala's *S27*; Peter Nichols' *Lingua Franca*, which transferred Off-Broadway; Dawn King's *Foxfinder*; and West End transfers for Joy Wilkinson's *Fair*; Nicholas de Jongh's *Plague Over England*; Jack Thorne's *Fanny and Faggot*; and Neil McPherson's *It Is Easy To Be Dead*. The late Miriam Karlin made her last stage appearance in *Many Roads to Paradise* in 2008.

UK premieres of foreign plays have included plays by Brad Fraser, Lanford Wilson, Larry Kramer, Tennessee Williams, the English premiere of Robert McLellan's Scots language classic, *Jamie the Saxt*; and three West End transfers – Frank McGuinnesss' *Gates of Gold* with William Gaunt and John Bennett; Joe DiPietro's *F***ing Men*; and Craig Higginson's *Dream of the Dog* with Dame Janet Suzman.

Rediscoveries of neglected work – most commissioned by the Finborough Theatre – have included the first London revivals of Rolf Hochhuth's *Soldiers* and *The Representative*; both parts of Keith Dewhurst's *Lark Rise to Candleford*; *The Women's War*, an evening of original suffragette plays; *Etta Jenks* with Clarke Peters and Daniela

Nardini; Noël Coward's first play, *The Rat Trap*; Charles Wood's *Jingo* with Susannah Harker; Emlyn Williams's *Accolade*; Lennox Robinson's *Drama at Inish* with Celia Imrie and Paul O'Grady; John Van Druten's *London Wall* which transferred to St James' Theatre; and J. B. Priestley's *Cornelius* which transferred to a sell out Off-Broadway run in New York City.

Music theatre has included the new (premieres from Grant Olding, Charles Miller, Michael John LaChuisa, Adam Guettel, Andrew Lippa, Paul Scott Goodman, and Adam Gwon's *Ordinary Days* which transferred to the West End) and the old (the UK premiere of Rodgers and Hammerstein's *State Fair* which also transferred to the West End, and the UK premiere of Jerry Herman's *The Grand Tour*), and the acclaimed 'Celebrating British Music Theatre' series.

The Finborough Theatre won The Stage Fringe Theatre of the Year Award in 2011, *London Theatre Reviews'* Empty Space Peter Brook Award in 2010 and 2012, the Empty Space Peter Brook Award's Dan Crawford Pub Theatre Award in 2005 and 2008, the Empty Space Peter Brook Mark Marvin Award in 2004, and swept the board with eight awards at the 2012 OffWestEnd Awards. It is the only unsubsidised theatre ever to be awarded the Channel 4 Playwrights Scheme bursary ten times.

www.finboroughtheatre.co.uk

FINBOROUGH | THEATRE

VIBRANT **NEW WRITING** | UNIQUE **REDISCOVERIES**
118 Finborough Road, London SW10 9ED
admin@finboroughtheatre.co.uk
www.finboroughtheatre.co.uk

The Finborough Theatre has the support of the Channel 4 Playwrights' Scheme, sponsored by Channel 4 Television and supported by The Peggy Ramsay Foundation.

The Finborough Theatre is a member of the Independent Theatre Council, the Society of Independent Theatres, Musical Theatre Network, The Friends of Brompton Cemetery and The Earl's Court Society
www.earlscourtsociety.org.uk

Supported by

Mailing
Email admin@finboroughtheatre.co.uk or give your details to our Box Office staff to join our free email list. If you would like to be sent a free season leaflet every three months, just include your postal address and postcode.

Feedback
We welcome your comments, complaints and suggestions. Write to Finborough Theatre, 118 Finborough Road, London SW10 9ED or email us at admin@finboroughtheatre.co.uk

Playscripts
Many of the Finborough Theatre's plays have been published and are on sale from our website.

On social media

    www.facebook.com/FinboroughTheatre

    www.twitter.com/finborough

    finboroughtheatre.tumblr.com

    www.instagram.com/finboroughtheatre

    www.youtube.com/user/finboroughtheatre

Friends
The Finborough Theatre is a registered charity. We receive no public funding, and rely solely on the support of our audiences. Please do consider supporting us by becoming a member of our Friends of the

Finborough Theatre scheme. There are four categories of Friends, each offering a wide range of benefits.

Richard Tauber Friends – Val Bond. James Brown. Tom Erhardt. Stephen and Jennifer Harper. Bill Hornby. Richard Jackson. Mike Lewendon. John Lawson. Harry MacAuslan. Mark and Susan Nichols. Sarah Thomas. Kathryn McDowall. Barry Serjent. Lavinia Webb. Stephen Winningham.

Lionel Monckton Friends – Philip G Hooker. Martin and Wendy Kramer. Deborah Milner. Maxine and Eric Reynolds.

William Terriss Friends – Stuart Ffoulkes. Leo and Janet Liebster. Paul and Lindsay Kennedy. Corinne Rooney. Jon and NoraLee Sedmak.

Smoking is not permitted in the auditorium and the use of cameras and recording equipment is strictly prohibited.

In accordance with the requirements of the Royal Borough of Kensington and Chelsea:
1. The public may leave at the end of the performance by all doors and such doors must at that time be kept open.
2. All gangways, corridors, staircases and external passageways intended for exit shall be left entirely free from obstruction whether permanent or temporary.
3. Persons shall not be permitted to stand or sit in any of the gangways intercepting the seating or to sit in any of the other gang-ways.

The Finborough Theatre is licensed by the Royal Borough of Kensington and Chelsea to The Steam Industry, a registered charity and a company limited by guarantee. Registered in England and Wales no. 3448268. Registered Charity no. 1071304. Registered Office: 118 Finborough Road, London SW10 9ED.

The Steam Industry was founded by Phil Willmott in 1992. It comprises two strands to its work: the Finborough Theatre (under Artistic Director Neil McPherson); and The Phil Willmott Company (under Artistic Director Phil Willmott) which presents productions throughout London as well as annually at the Finborough Theatre.

DUBAILAND

by Carmen Nasr

⅃SAMUEL FRENCH⅃

samuelfrench.co.uk

Cover image: Eliot Nathan

THINKING ABOUT PERFORMING A SHOW?

There are thousands of plays and musicals available to perform from Samuel French right now, and applying for a licence is easier and more affordable than you might think

From classic plays to brand new musicals, from monologues to epic dramas, there are shows for everyone.

Plays and musicals are protected by copyright law so if you want to perform them, the first thing you'll need is a licence. This simple process helps support the playwright by ensuring they get paid for their work, and means that you'll have the documents you need to stage the show in public.

Not all our shows are available to perform all the time, so it's important to check and apply for a licence before you start rehearsals or commit to doing the show.

LEARN MORE & FIND THOUSANDS OF SHOWS

Browse our full range of plays and musicals and find out more about how to license a show
www.samuelfrench.co.uk/perform

Talk to the friendly experts in our Licensing team for advice on choosing a show, and help with licensing
plays@samuelfrench.co.uk   020 7387 9373

Acting Editions

BORN TO PERFORM

Playscripts designed from the ground up to work the way you do in rehearsal, performance and study

---

Larger, clearer text for easier reading

Wider margins for notes

Performance features such as character and props lists, sound and lighting cues, and more

---

+ CHOOSE A SIZE AND STYLE TO SUIT YOU

  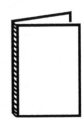

STANDARD EDITION

Our regular paperback book at our regular size

SPIRAL-BOUND EDITION

The same size as the Standard Edition, but with a sturdy, easy-to-fold, easy-to-hold spiral-bound spine

LARGE EDITION

A4 size and spiral bound, with larger text and a blank page for notes opposite every page of text. Perfect for technical and directing use

ABOUT THE AUTHOR

Carmen Nasr is a British-Lebanese playwright, and is currently Channel 4 Playwrights Scheme Playwright in Residence at the Finborough Theatre, supported by the Peggy Ramsay Foundation. *Dubailand* received a staged reading at *Vibrant 2015 – A Festival of Finborough Playwrights*. Her first play *The House of My Father* received a staged reading at *Vibrant 2014 – A Festival of Finborough Playwrights* and was also part of the annual Nour Festival of Contemporary Middle Eastern and North African Art and Culture. In 2015, *The House of My Father* was longlisted for the Bruntwood Prize, and in 2015 she was shortlisted for the OffWestEnd Adopt a Playwright Award.

AUTHOR'S NOTE

As part of the play's development, a number of people agreed to meet with me and be interviewed in Dubai. Without their openness and generosity, the play wouldn't have been written. I would like to thank each of you: Rita Tohme, Dona Varghese, James Munt, Omar Fakhouri, Wassim Fakhouri and Tala Itani.

I would also like to thank Susie Safavi, for not only jumping on a plane to Dubai with me at the last minute, but for believing in the play before I'd even written a single word. Thank you to Neil McPherson and the Finborough Theatre for nurturing my work. Thank you Dan Rebellato for teaching me things, which some people might believe are unteachable.

Thank you Sergio, Sou-Sou, Ezzo, Mum and Dad for all your support.

For Rosie and Lily

MUSIC USE NOTE

Licensees are solely responsible for obtaining formal written permission from copyright owners to use copyrighted music in the performance of this play and are strongly cautioned to do so. If no such permission is obtained by the licensee, then the licensee must use only original music that the licensee owns and controls. Licensees are solely responsible and liable for all music clearances and shall indemnify the copyright owners of the play(s) and their licensing agent, Samuel French, against any costs, expenses, losses and liabilities arising from the use of music by licensees. Please contact the appropriate music licensing authority in your territory for the rights to any incidental music.

USE OF COPYRIGHT MUSIC

A licence issued by Samuel French Ltd to perform this play does not include permission to use the incidental music specified in this copy. Where the place of performance is already licensed by the PERFORMING RIGHT SOCIETY (PRS) a return of the music used must be made to them. If the place of performance is not so licensed then application should be made to the PRS, 2 Pancras Square, London, N1C 4AG (www.mcps-prs-alliance.co.uk)

A separate and additional licence from PHONOGRAPHIC PERFORMANCE LTD, 1 Upper James Street, London W1F 9DE (www.ppluk.com) is needed whenever commercial recordings are used

Duabiland was first performed at the Finborough Theatre on Sunday, 5 February 2017 with the following cast:

Amar	**Adi Chugh**
Clara	**Mitzli Rose Neville**
Tanveer	**Varun Sharma**
Tommie	**Leon Williams**
Amanda	**Belinda Stewart-Wilson**
Deena	**Reena Lalbihari**
Jamie	**Nicholas Banks**
Lali	**Aanya Chadha**

Director	**Georgie Staight**
Designer	**Bex Kemp**
Lighting Designer	**Robbie Butler**
Sound Designer	**Jack Burton**
Stage Manager / Assistant Director	**Wiebke Green**
Producer	**Caley Powell**

CHARACTERS

AMAR . . . . Male, 30s, Indian
CLARA. . . . . Female, 30s, Indian
TANVEER. . . . . Male, 20s, Indian
JAMIE . . . . Male, 30s, British
TOMMIE. . . . . .Male, 40s, British
DEENA . . . . Female, 30s, Indian
AMANDA . . . . .Female, early 50s, British
LALI. . . . . Female, 8-years-old, Indian

WAITER / TAXI DRIVER*

AIRPORT OFFICIAL**
CAMP OFFICIAL**
GOVERNMENT OFFICIAL**

*Played by the same actor playing Amar or Tanveer
** Played by the same actor playing Tanveer

Scene 1

The Dubai skyline at dusk. Its geometry is only just beginning to shimmer and sparkle, the abundance of skyscrapers is at once exciting and menacing.

AMAR, a construction worker in his early thirties, Indian, stands on the 88th floor of an unfinished skyscraper in Business Bay. He is surrounded by lights, which sometimes look like stars. He is wearing his work clothes: blue overalls and safety helmet. He is looking out towards the sky, towards the sea, towards the past. He looks straight out at the audience.

AMAR My little one, my darling. Can you see the lights – the lights sparkling in the sky of the world? People think they're stars but they're not

Lights. They're lights. Lights in all the buildings hundreds and thousands of them

This is the future my darling. Isn't it pretty?

Can you see me? Can you see me standing here in the stars? Look at me I'm in the future. Can you believe it? I'm in the future and I'm building one of the highest buildings, in the best city in the world

Everything here is beautiful. And you know what? It's true there are 200 flavours of ice cream in every shop

What's that my darling? Of course I'll bring you here one day. Yes ice cream, we'll have ice cream in the stars

Scene 2

The security area of a German airport, maybe Frankfurt or Düsseldorf. Everything is clean, minimal and under control. CLARA *and an* AIRPORT SECURITY OFFICIAL *are standing over an open suitcase.* CLARA, *a journalist, is in her early thirties, British. The* AIRPORT SECURITY OFFICIAL *remains cool and collected throughout the scene.* CLARA *does not.*

AIRPORT SECURITY It's impossible

CLARA What?

AIRPORT SECURITY It's against the official regulations

CLARA It's a bar of chocolate

AIRPORT SECURITY It violates the maximum allowance of 100 millilitres of fluids

CLARA You having a laugh?

AIRPORT SECURITY Excuse me?

CLARA You having a laugh? You joking?

AIRPORT SECURITY I'm certainly not miss

CLARA It's a chocolate bar

AIRPORT It violates/the maximum –

CLARA It's solid

AIRPORT SECURITY Yes I agree it's solid, but –

CLARA But what?

AIRPORT SECURITY It's the marzipan

CLARA The what?

AIRPORT SECURITY The marzipan

CLARA What's wrong with the marzipan?

AIRPORT SECURITY It's not a solid

CLARA It's not a liquid

AIRPORT SECURITY It's well it's...sort of soft

CLARA Soft?

AIRPORT SECURITY Yes. It's classified as a fluid in this airport

CLARA Well that's a little bit ridiculous

AIRPORT SECURITY Please miss don't raise your voice like that

CLARA I didn't raise my - *(in a lower volume)* I didn't raise my voice

A flight announcement is heard in the background during the next few lines in English, German and Arabic.

ANNOUNCER Final passengers for Emirates Airline flight 506 to Dubai please make your way to gate 88. Final passengers for Emirates Airline flight 506 to Dubai please make your way to gate 88.

CLARA Listen that's my flight, I'm gonna / miss it

AIRPORT SECURITY Unfortunately you must leave the item here

CLARA No way, this is bloody ridiculous. Bloody Germans

AIRPORT SECURITY Please be careful with your words miss You must leave the item here

CLARA Christ. Listen this thing cost ten euros. Ten euros for a chocolate bar and you want me to chuck it away?

AIRPORT SECURITY You must leave the item here

CLARA No

AIRPORT SECURITY Then I will have to call security

CLARA You are security

AIRPORT SECURITY More security

Another flight announcement is heard in the background

CLARA For Christ's sake

AIRPORT SECURITY Place the chocolate bar in the bin

CLARA No

AIRPORT SECURITY Place it in the bin

CLARA No

AIRPORT SECURITY I'm going to have to call / more –

CLARA Call them. Call all the bloody security in the goddam airport. I paid for this, for this marzipan chocolate bar. This is my chocolate bar. I worked hard for this chocolate bar. I have earned this chocolate bar. It's my property

AIRPORT SECURITY Place the chocolate in the bin

CLARA No

AIRPORT SECURITY Then I can't let you through to your flight

CLARA Jesus Christ I'm gonna miss my flight

AIRPORT SECURITY Miss, place the chocolate bar in the bin

A pause. She considers leaving it. She stares at the security officer. She slowly opens the chocolate bar and begins to eat it. She chews slowly and deliberately at first, but gradually she eats faster and faster until she is struggling to stuff the chocolate into her mouth. She starts to gag, there is chocolate smeared on her face, some of it falls to the floor. She is determined to keep going. It takes some time, but she finishes the chocolate bar.

Scene 3

AMAR and TANVEER sit in a canteen in the middle of the desert. They are having their evening meal after work. The glimmering skyline is tiny in the distance.

AMAR What do you have?

TANVEER Fish

AMAR I only have potatoes

TANVEER I have fish

AMAR Yes I know you just told me

TANVEER It looks good doesn't it
Why didn't you get any fish?

AMAR It must have finished

TANVEER Bad luck

AMAR Bad luck

They eat in silence.

Is the fish good?

TANVEER It's good

AMAR What does it taste like?

TANVEER The sea

Pause.

Do you want some?

AMAR No thank you

TANVEER It's a little overcooked

AMAR Everything is overcooked

TANVEER It's dry

AMAR The pan has to be very hot

TANVEER What?

AMAR When you fry fish the pan has to be very hot or else it
takes a long time to cook and then the fish, well it gets dry

TANVEER My wife is a great cook

AMAR Is she?

TANVEER Wonderful
It doesn't taste the same does it, the flesh, the flesh of the fish

AMAR It doesn't taste real

TANVEER Where are you?

AMAR Business Bay

TANVEER Me too. Which one?

AMAR Vision Tower

TANVEER Falcon Tower

AMAR How many floors left?

TANVEER Thirty-six. You?

AMAR Ninety-one

TANVEER How many more months?

AMAR Twenty-nine

TANVEER Twenty-three
Passport?

AMAR What do you think?

TANVEER Are the potatoes good?

AMAR Not bad. Crispy skin

TANVEER Nice

AMAR Anybody?

    Anybody today?

TANVEER Just one

AMAR Fall?

TANVEER Yeah

AMAR What floor

TANVEER Fifty-four

AMAR Alive

TANVEER No

    Unlucky

AMAR Or stupid

    Beat.

TANVEER My friend told me that they're building a cricket field in his camp

AMAR A real one?

TANVEER Why what other kind is there?

AMAR You know what I mean

TANVEER Yes a real one

    And they have their own kitchens

AMAR Where is it?

TANVEER Not far from here

AMAR How did he get a place?

    TANVEER *looks around, making sure he can't be overheard.*

TANVEER He knows a guy, who knows a guy

AMAR Can you find out

TANVEER What?

AMAR How he did it

TANVEER It's impossible

Do you want the last piece?

AMAR Alright

He eats the last piece of fish.

It's disgusting

TANVEER I know

AMAR It doesn't taste like the sea, the sea tastes good

TANVEER It's impossible

AMAR What is?

TANVEER To change camp

AMAR What about with money?

TANVEER Who has money?

AMAR True

TANVEER Well, there is

AMAR What?

TANVEER Do you want a tea?

AMAR No. Say what you were going to say

TANVEER There is you know one way to change, to change camp. But

AMAR But

TANVEER It's worse than money

AMAR What can be worse than money?

TANVEER Information

Scene 4

An office in Dubai's Media City district. It is on the 114th floor of a skyscraper. There is a large amount of glass and we can see buildings everywhere. A picture of Dubai's ruler Sheikh Mohammed bin Rashid Al Maktoum hangs on the wall. TOMMIE *stands alone. He is in his late thirties, British. He wears a suit and is well groomed.*

TOMMIE Opening image. The world, spinning. It's a stunning sexy world, all blue and green shimmer - it's luminous. We hear the beat, the beat of violin strings, a dozen, no damn it, a hundred violin strings softly going ba bam ba bam ba bam ba bam

One hundred violin strings start to play softly.

Then swoosh, classic zoom, all the way through the atmosphere, stratmosphere whatever it's bloody called - down to the sparkling sprawl of DUBAI. We slow down and hover in the sky - an Arabian falcon sweeps across the front of the camera and we glide down on the ancient pulsing muscle of his wings, the violins kick it up a gear, the cellos start having a go bum bu bum bu bum bu bum bu bum bu bum bu bum

We hear the sound of cellos joining the violins.

And then, oh just look at it - a forest of skyscrapers in the vastness of an arid desert. Steel glass steel glass more steel more glass.

Everything clean. Everything sharp. A beat kicks in, a bit electro, a bit techno, a bit chill out lounge pish pish pish pish pish pish pish pish pish

A soft beat joins the violins and the cellos.

An Emirati riding a stallion through the desert in slow motion, the skyline of Dubai in the distance, close-up on particles of sand flying off its hooves, the white headdress flowing in the wind –

Voiceover: *Own the lifestyle of a lifetime*

The beat picks up badabadabadabadabadabadabadabadabada

The beat picks up.

Shot of the tallest building in the world, giant jets of water shoot out of a gigantic fountain schwoop schwoop schwoop. Close-up of some young Emirati kids staring at the pulsating jets in wonder. *(He mimicks their gasps)* The palm island from above, an ocean view hallucination, zoom down – swiiiissshhhhhhh – luxury beach house – a Western couple walk along their private beach holding hands. A shot of the sparkling sea, the setting sun – they look at the sky and laugh

Voiceover: *Invest in life, invest in choice, invest in you*

An Enya style, ethnic new age singing comes in and straddles the beat as it picks up – tikatikatikatikatikati katikatikatikatikatikatikatika

An Enya-style singing is added to the music, the beat quickens, as does TOMMIE.

The beach in all its white-sanded glory. A palm tree reflected in the windscreen of a moving car. A man swings a golf club. An Emirati couple having dinner, he talks – she laughs. Fireworks cascade down skyscrapers. More buildings. More fireworks. A crowd cheers. South Asian construction workers smile for a group photo, they pump their fists in triumph. The silhouette of a million cranes lit up by the setting sun. A group of Emiratis shake hands with European men in suits. Everybody smiles

Two glamorous women jump into an infinity pool on the rooftop of a skyscraper. Time lapse of Dubai Mall. A child licks an ice cream and smiles. The whole skyline, sparkling, dazzling, all the lights sped up like a galaxy of stars Suddenly the peace of the desert, the man on the stallion gallops across the screen in slow motion. He comes to a stop, he looks out at the city – his city – bathed in the setting sun. Close up of his eyes, full of ancient wisdom. He smiles

Voiceover: *Welcome to Dubai. Welcome to the skyline of your dreams*

A pause.

We now notice that AMANDA, *early fifties, British,* DEENA *late twenties, Indian, and* JAMIE *have been watching* TOMMIE.

AMANDA Oh Tommie, you are just – wonderful Tommie, it's just aghhhhhh, you know? It's fantastic – no it's invigorating. Deena?

DEENA What?

AMANDA Any thoughts?

DEENA *hesitates. There is a pause.*

DEENA I don't like the hawk

TOMMIE It's a falcon

DEENA Falcon whatever I don't like the falcon

TOMMIE How can you not like the falcon?

JAMIE I love the falcon Tommie

TOMMIE And why do you love the falcon Jamie?

JAMIE In general or in the context of the video?

TOMMIE The video mate

JAMIE Well it's a very majestic creature / and it's a symbol of

AMANDA Deena why don't you like the bird?

TOMMIE It's a symbol / of –

DEENA Of antiquated Arab traditions

TOMMIE Tradition, heritage exactly

DEENA That's why I don't like it, it's antiquated, it's old, it's stagnant. Dubai is the opposite – the Arabs are building the future – give them some bloody credit – so they have a thing for falcons, but they've also built a modern metropolis in the middle of a desert in the same time it takes you to upgrade a bloody railway line in the UK

TOMMIE It's an homage to the ancient traditions of the Emiratis – and I can assure you Amanda that the Emirati shareholders upstairs will be all over that / falcon –

DEENA The Emiratis Tommie, figured out a long time ago that Europeans don't want to buy a property somewhere Arab – they don't want falcons and angry brown men roaming the desert on / wild stallions –

TOMMIE What do they want?

DEENA They want to see westernised tame Arabs riding golden Lamborghinis, veiled women slurping frappachinos. They want to spread their legs wide across the artificial white sand, look out at the skyscrapers and think – Christ I can't believe I'm in the Middle East

JAMIE Isn't that pretty much what everyone wants

DEENA Exactly no one wants arid deserts with vicious birds circling overhead

JAMIE I still like the falcon

DEENA No Jamie you like Tommie, that's why you like the hawk

TOMMIE Falcon

DEENA Falcon. Everything else was great – just get rid of the bird

TOMMIE Amanda?

AMANDA Get rid of it. You see Dubai's success comes from the ingenious idea of shearing away the qualities that define it as Arab. Desert? Build on it. Nomads? Give them a villa. Ban on alcohol? Scrap it. The falcon is just too well... Arab

TOMMIE No falcon

DEENA Oh and...

TOMMIE And what?

DEENA The stallion?

TOMMIE What about the bloody stallion Deena?

DEENA It has to go

TOMMIE Oh come on

JAMIE I have to say I love the stallion

DEENA Of course you do Jamie. Of course you love the bloody stallion

So instead of the shitty stallion bit at the end, what about this

DEENA *stands.*

The music heard previously starts to play.

A group of Emiratis shake hands with European men in suits Everybody smiles. Two glamorous women dive into a swimming pool on the roof of a skyscraper. Two Emirati men glide through a mall, they look like swans with takeaway Starbucks coffees. A yacht gently eases through the Marina as a couple watch it pass by from the balcony of their penthouse on the 88th floor. They look out at the breathtaking skyline bathed in the setting sun, they look at each other and smile, a little girl runs up from behind, her father scoops her up into his arms and points at the lights of the skyline that begin to resemble a sea of glimmering stars.

Voiceover: *Welcome to Dubai. Welcome to the future*

AMANDA Get rid of the stallion Tommie

TOMMIE I just...fine

AMANDA We're trying to sell property here not make a Western

TOMMIE Absolutely

AMANDA Jamie

JAMIE Amanda

AMANDA Have you finished the report on the market research?

JAMIE Yes

AMANDA Learn anything?

JAMIE There's an anxiety

AMANDA An anxiety

JAMIE Yes an anxiety about buying something that remains intangible for so long

TOMMIE Jesus people are so wanky

JAMIE But this concept that they're not just buying a property – but an actual piece of the future, made them very excited. And the promotional videos went down a treat Tommie

TOMMIE Thanks mate

JAMIE They love Dubai, I mean people really love Dubai –

It's like there's been a collective realisation that nowhere else in the world can you live like this and now everyone wants a piece

AMANDA So what's the bloody problem then?

JAMIE Well they need something to keep them entertained, ease the anxiety until the property is actually / built

DEENA We already put out a quarterly email up-date on all pre-purchased construction projects

JAMIE They need something more immediate, more accessible – interactive – something more Dubai

AMANDA Such as?

JAMIE Well I've had an idea

Beat.

AMANDA Yes?

JAMIE A live feed – twenty-four hours of footage streamed live from the construction site

AMANDA *thinks.*

AMANDA I like it Jamie. I like it a lot

JAMIE People can log in and watch their future apartment or penthouse or whatever being built brick by brick

AMANDA Deena

DEENA What?

AMANDA Any thoughts?

Beat.

DEENA It's clever

AMANDA It is clever isn't it – carry on Jamie

JAMIE We could have cameras dotted all around the site, inside rooms, on balconies, from the tops of cranes, even people's helmets

AMANDA And people can swap between views

JAMIE Exactly – they locate the part of the building where their flat will be and see the skyline from their future Dubai balcony from their sofa in Dorset, from their living room in Munich

AMANDA No more anxiety

JAMIE And less anxiety means more / sales

AMANDA It can't be *live* live of course

JAMIE Why not?

AMANDA Well because there may be things we want to edit out

JAMIE Such as?

AMANDA Well, such as the odd minor health and safety violation, a misplaced cup of boiling tea, a mislaid hammer tripping someone up, that kind of nonsense. No construction site is perfect no matter how much regulation you throw at it

JAMIE Right of course

AMANDA We'll edit it first, just to be safe

JAMIE Then it goes out "live"

AMANDA Don't worry they won't know the difference. Let's trial it on a current project, test the waters. Business Bay?

JAMIE Perfect

AMANDA Tommie can you get on to tech to set it all up and Jamie you can be in charge of editing

JAMIE Absolutely

AMANDA Great work everyone

AMANDA *exits.* DEENA *follows her.*

A short silence passes.

JAMIE I loved the falcon

TOMMIE Me too

JAMIE And the stallion

TOMMIE Cheers mate

Scene 5

Eighty-eighth floor of Vision Towers. **AMAR** *is standing on the edge of the roof. A* **CAMP OFFICIAL** *appears.*

CAMP OFFICIAL The rules

AMAR Yes the rules

CAMP OFFICIAL Anyone?

AMAR Anyone

CAMP OFFICIAL You know

AMAR I don't

CAMP OFFICIAL Breaking them?

AMAR It's impossible

CAMP OFFICIAL What's impossible?

AMAR To break them

CAMP OFFICIAL Break what?

AMAR The rules

CAMP OFFICIAL Is it?

AMAR Impossible. Almost. Yes

CAMP OFFICIAL What about action

AMAR Action?

CAMP OFFICIAL Is there talk –

AMAR Talk of what –

CAMP OFFICIAL Of action

AMAR What kind of action?

CAMP OFFICIAL The bad kind

AMAR What's the good kind?

CAMP OFFICIAL Good / kind?

AMAR The good kind of action?

Beat.

CAMP OFFICIAL Work

AMAR Work. Of course / work

CAMP OFFICIAL And the bad kind?

AMAR Of action?

CAMP OFFICIAL Yes

AMAR I don't know

CAMP OFFICIAL Large gatherings

AMAR Gatherings

CAMP OFFICIAL Big plans

AMAR Plans

CAMP OFFICIAL Big demands

AMAR Demands

CAMP OFFICIAL And

AMAR And

CAMP OFFICIAL *(whispers)* strikes

AMAR *(whispers)* strikes

CAMP OFFICIAL Then riots

AMAR Riots?

CAMP OFFICIAL Then

AMAR Then?

CAMP OFFICIAL So. Any talk?

AMAR *thinks.*

AMAR No. nothing

CAMP OFFICIAL Nothing

AMAR Nothing

CAMP OFFICIAL At all

AMAR At all

CAMP OFFICIAL Information is better than money

AMAR What will it get me?

CAMP OFFICIAL What will what get you?

AMAR Information. What will it / get me?

CAMP OFFICIAL What do you want?

AMAR *hesitates.*

AMAR My passport

CAMP OFFICIAL Difficult

AMAR Camp

CAMP OFFICIAL Camp?

AMAR Change

CAMP OFFICIAL Change camp

AMAR Yes

CAMP OFFICIAL Maybe

AMAR Cricket field?

CAMP OFFICIAL Green

AMAR Shower?

CAMP OFFICIAL Hot

AMAR Bed?

CAMP OFFICIAL Soft

AMAR Fish

CAMP OFFICIAL Fresh

AMAR Floor

CAMP OFFICIAL Shiny

AMAR Tea

CAMP OFFICIAL Chamomile

AMAR TV

CAMP OFFICIAL Flat

AMAR Room

CAMP OFFICIAL Light

AMAR Glass

CAMP OFFICIAL Steel

AMAR Falcon

CAMP OFFICIAL Angry

AMAR Future

CAMP OFFICIAL City

AMAR Sun

CAMP OFFICIAL Warm

AMAR Boss

CAMP OFFICIAL Friend

AMAR Roof

CAMP OFFICIAL Swimming pool

AMAR Passport

CAMP OFFICIAL Home

AMAR Money

CAMP OFFICIAL Father

AMAR Coffee

CAMP OFFICIAL Mother

AMAR Ice cream

CAMP OFFICIAL Stars

AMAR Love

CAMP OFFICIAL Lali

Scene 6

Dubai Mall. **CLARA** *sits at a table in a coffee shop with* **JAMIE**. *Everything is marble, airy and light. It's buzzing and calm all at once.* **CLARA** *is very observant and aware of her surroundings; she has a notebook and pen.*

CLARA Your beard!

JAMIE Oh yeah, you know it's the desert and that

CLARA Huh?

JAMIE It's too hot

CLARA Oh right. How do you feel without it?

JAMIE Like a fucking child actually

CLARA Yeah I see what you mean

JAMIE Oh / cheers

CLARA What? I was a big fan of the beard!

JAMIE You've always got it in for / me

CLARA Oh stop it, you know I'm teasing

JAMIE Do I really look like a child?

Beat.

CLARA Actually you're looking really well, you're all tanned and – have you been exercising?

JAMIE Everyone works out in Dubai

CLARA Why?

JAMIE Because you tan all year round on the beach – you gotta look good

CLARA scribbles something down in her notebook.

CLARA That's / hilarious

JAMIE Did you just make a note of that? Why the hell are you making notes?

CLARA Don't be so nosy Jamie – it's private

JAMIE Is it for the magazine?

CLARA Do you want a coffee?

    CLARA signals to the WAITER.

JAMIE Yeah Americano. With hot milk on the side

CLARA Since when do you have hot milk on the side?

JAMIE Since I realised that

    I can have whatever I want

They look at each other for what feels like a little bit too long. They are interrupted by the WAITER.

WAITER Good afternoon

CLARA Two Americanos please

JAMIE With hot milk on the side

WAITER Something else?

CLARA Can I ask you a question?

WAITER Yes

CLARA Are you happy here?

WAITER Very happy

CLARA Do you like living in Dubai?

WAITER Yes it's wonderful

CLARA How much money do you earn?

WAITER Excuse me?

CLARA You know every month how much do you get paid?

WAITER I understand, I don't know, each month different

JAMIE Clara

CLARA On average

WAITER I'm sorry I don't know / the –

CLARA Alright never mind, don't worry

Are you in a relationship?

WAITER Relationship?

CLARA Are you married?

WAITER No not married. Very good. Two Americano and hot milk on the side, anything else?

He exits.

JAMIE Jesus Clara what the hell was that?

CLARA Research

JAMIE It was bloody rude is what it was

CLARA *makes some notes.*

Why do you keep writing shit down?

CLARA It's for work

JAMIE I thought you were covering the Dubai Shopping Festival or something

CLARA I am. This is...something else

Talking of work – how's your job?

JAMIE Amazing. It's ace.

CLARA Construction company right?

JAMIE Yeah

CLARA Laying bricks?

JAMIE Very funny

CLARA Well what do you do?

JAMIE I'm – get this – a Creative Digital PR Specialist

CLARA What does that even mean?

JAMIE That I'm special

CLARA Do you make them look shiny and clean?

JAMIE They are shiny and clean

CLARA Do you wear a suit to work?

JAMIE Yeah

CLARA I bet you look good in it

JAMIE I've got a confession to make

CLARA What?

JAMIE I bought some loafers the other day

CLARA Oh no Jamie – not loafers! What are you turning into?

Beat.

JAMIE Why did you never call?

CLARA I called you yesterday

JAMIE It's been a year

CLARA I know I –

JAMIE I thought that...after you and Matt split up that you'd call me, I waited

CLARA I needed some time to, some space to – you / know

JAMIE Well anyway – look it's really good to see you Clara

CLARA You too Jamie

Beat.

So what's it like living here?

JAMIE It's crazy awesome, it's insane

CLARA Insane?

JAMIE I didn't know life could be this bloody great

CLARA Jesus I must be missing / out then

JAMIE On Fridays right, there's this thing called brunch

CLARA I know what brunch is Jamie

JAMIE No no this is different. Brunch in Dubai is not brunch as you know it Clara. Every Friday, Jesus it's mental – you pay a fixed fee and between twelve and four, it's unlimited booze, unlimited food

CLARA Wow

JAMIE The first time I went a few weeks back

It was at a huge hotel on the palm island, feels like you're out right in the middle of the sea – it's nuts

So we go into this hotel, walk down these gigantic marble stairs, through the biggest aquarium tunnel in the world, and there are all these mad animal creatures

CLARA Like what?

JAMIE Like white sharks, giant squid, baby seahorses all these magical sea creatures – and weird sea urchin things all floating about – anyway at the end of the marble stairs, there's these waiter boys in tuxes plying you with glasses of champagne, then you go inside and it's all opulence, chandeliers, huge pillars all that kind of stuff

The music's pumping

CLARA What kind of music?

JAMIE Electro techno that kinda stuff and everyone all dressed up, you get civilised brunches, but this was like...party brunch

CLARA Good food?

JAMIE Oh the food. The food is crazy – lobster, sushi, scallops, mental types of exotic fish, all different cuisines piles and piles of it. There's even a whole room just for the cheese

And the booze, you can have whatever you want champagne, cocktails, its on tap. We got totally wasted.

Anyway there's always some sort of entertainment, like a magician or a dancer or performing animals or something like that, this time they had all these easels set up outside so that people could go and paint and shit

So we go outside and there's this girl and she's painting a turtle

CLARA Was she drunk?

JAMIE Drunk? She was completely twatted

So I go up to her and I'm like do you want some help I'm a classically trained artist and she hands me her brush and I walk over to her turtle canvas and draw a big massive cock over it

JAMIE *bursts out laughing.*

CLARA Jesus who are you?

JAMIE What? It's funny

CLARA It sounds like the kinda thing you would hate

JAMIE Well turns out I was wrong. It's ace

CLARA Do you go every Friday?

JAMIE Yeah most weeks and the rest of the weekend everybody stumbles around in a numb hangover, all you can do is lie on the beach, soak up the sun. It's awesome

Beat.

Where are you staying I didn't ask?

CLARA The magazine put me up in a shitty hotel in Deira

JAMIE You can always crash at mine if you want, I've got this ridiculous flat, it's like a Manhattan penthouse overlooking the Marina

CLARA I hope that was a genuine offer because I just might take you / up on it

JAMIE Shit it's Friday tomorrow you want to come and have brunch with / me?

CLARA Jamie, do you ever work on site?

JAMIE What site?

Beat.

CLARA The construction sites, do you ever go down and work on site?

JAMIE No why would I? I mean I've had a couple of tours and that - why are you asking?

CLARA Well, I thought you could help me

JAMIE With what?

CLARA My work. My research

JAMIE For the magazine?

CLARA No not the shitty magazine and the shitty shopping festival - real work

I want to be taken seriously Jamie, you know the magazine was always just a way to get my foot in the door

JAMIE You've worked there for years now

CLARA I'm a journalist Jamie. I want to write about things that you know matter. I've got to take advantage of being here

JAMIE Why here?

CLARA Because of the workers

JAMIE What workers?

CLARA The labourers, the construction workers

JAMIE What about them?

CLARA Don't pretend you don't know what I'm talking about

JAMIE I'm not pretending

CLARA Conditions, contracts you know all that stuff

A brief pause.

JAMIE Look I know what you're getting at, yeah their wages are really low but –

CLARA I know that you know

JAMIE The money they earn here is nowhere near what they could ever dream of earning back home

CLARA Is that what your company told you?

JAMIE No everybody knows – google it

CLARA What about the deaths?

JAMIE Accidental deaths on construction sites are pretty standard Clara, it happens all over the world, it's a dangerous job

CLARA Not on this scale

JAMIE Put your voice down a bit

CLARA Why?

JAMIE Cause you're shouting, it's rude to shout in public here

CLARA Jamie I'm serious about this. These people, their story has to be told

JAMIE What story?

CLARA The workers' story

JAMIE There is no story Clara

CLARA I thought you of all people would care

JAMIE Care about what?

CLARA Their plight

JAMIE Hold on, what do you think is actually happening here?

CLARA These men, these men are desperately poor, desperate for a job, they get approached by agents back in their villages who promise them jobs in Dubai with monthly salaries they could only dream of and then when / they actually get here

JAMIE I genuinely don't know what you're talking / about

CLARA What's going on here is intolerable

JAMIE Is it really?

CLARA Yes Jamie it is

JAMIE And what are you planning to do about / it?

CLARA Expose it, make a racket, get people stirred up

JAMIE What's it for – a blog?

CLARA Don't be so patronising. I've got a contact at a national paper

JAMIE What and no contacts here?

CLARA I didn't know I would be sent out here until last week, I didn't have / the time

JAMIE And you want me to help you?

CLARA I want you to help me

JAMIE You want me to help you how?

CLARA I need to see where they work, maybe get some interviews / with them

JAMIE I can't do that Clara

CLARA But why Jamie?

JAMIE Because I can't

CLARA Why not?

JAMIE Because number one I'm not putting my job on the line for your vanity project, and number two I don't even know what you're banging on about

CLARA Since when did you stop giving a shit about the world? Jamie you used to care – it was you who would drag me out of bed to go to marches, it was you / who would –

JAMIE Yeah well I grew up Clara and I realised that it's not all good and bad, them and us – things are more complex than that

CLARA What kind of bubble are you living in?

JAMIE It's a bloody goldmine for them. They wouldn't even be here if it wasn't financially viable

CLARA Is that what all the other expats tell you at your piss-up brunches?

JAMIE Oh grow up Clara

CLARA You've changed so much

JAMIE I got tired of losing

CLARA What does it feel like to be winning?

JAMIE It feels fucking great

Scene 7

AMAR and TANVEER *sit on the edge of a building, engulfed by the multicoloured lights of the skyline. Large birds fly overhead.*

TANVEER Angry

AMAR Who

TANVEER Us

AMAR Us?

TANVEER Everyone. Everyone is angry

AMAR How angry?

TANVEER Very angry

AMAR Why?

TANVEER Why? Don't be stupid. You know why

   Beat.

AMAR I caught a pigeon

TANVEER What?

AMAR I caught a pigeon. It's a kind of bird

TANVEER I know what a pigeon is

AMAR Well I caught one

TANVEER How? Where?

AMAR At work

TANVEER On site?

AMAR On the seventy-sixth floor

The shift was almost done. Sun setting. There was an unusual
breeze. Then I saw a falcon. No not just one, there were
three or four. They were circling each other. Real beauties

TANVEER You know they use them to hunt the pigeons. They're
pests

They shit all over the buildings

AMAR So I saw these falcons. Circling and circling. They were
circling around a pigeon, and the pigeon was getting tired
it was flying all over the place, zigzagging and then – it
spotted me and it, well it started to fly towards me

TANVEER What did you do?

AMAR I stood on the edge and I held my arms out

TANVEER Did it come?

AMAR It flew straight into my arms

TANVEER And then?

AMAR And then

It was still

TANVEER What did the falcons do?

AMAR They hovered. They watched from a distance

TANVEER And the pigeon?

AMAR It was still, but it was panting

TANVEER Like a dog?

AMAR Yes a bit like a dog

I stroked its head. Gently. I stroked it and stroked it until
its panting, its panting turned to purring

TANVEER Like a cat

AMAR Yes a bit like a cat

I held it in front of my face. Like this

It opened its eyes and looked straight at me

With these black little dotty eyes

TANVEER   Like the eyes on a prawn

AMAR   Exactly

TANVEER   And the falcons?

AMAR   They were circling closer and closer

TANVEER   What did you do?

AMAR   I looked the pigeon in the eyes. It looked back

Beat.

Then I snapped its neck

Beat.

TANVEER   Why?

AMAR   Because I didn't want the falcons to win

Beat.

TANVEER   There's a gathering

AMAR   Of what?

TANVEER   Of...us

AMAR   Us?

TANVEER   Us – the men working on Business Bay

AMAR   When?

TANVEER   Thursday morning. As soon as we arrive to work, we refuse to enter the sites and gather together

AMAR   Gather where?

TANVEER   Shh

Outside Falcon Tower

AMAR   Thursday morning?

TANVEER Thursday morning

AMAR What are we going to do there?

TANVEER Demand

AMAR Demand what?

TANVEER What's ours

Scene 8

*JAMIE is in a taxi on Dubai's Sheikh Zayed Road, it is
late. The lights of the skyscrapers rise and fall colouring
the car's interior. The TAXI DRIVER wears a uniform,
a white shirt, waistcoat and black trousers. JAMIE has
had a lot to drink.*

TAXI DRIVER You are British?

JAMIE Excuse me?

TAXI DRIVER You are British?

JAMIE Yes

TAXI DRIVER May I ask you a question?

JAMIE OK

TAXI DRIVER British people, why they always cry after a night
out?

JAMIE Do they?

TAXI DRIVER Many customers, British customers when they go
home at night from the bar or the hotels, they are drunk.
Here in my taxi, they cry

JAMIE Well that's embarrassing

TAXI DRIVER I didn't understand and I thought maybe you
understood

JAMIE No I don't think I understand either sorry

Beat.

I don't know maybe they're tired

TAXI DRIVER Tired?

JAMIE Tired of their life, or maybe they miss their country

Beat.

TAXI DRIVER I haven't seen my family for three years

JAMIE That's a long time

TAXI DRIVER In six month my contract finish and I go home and I will never come back

JAMIE You don't want to come back to Dubai?

TAXI DRIVER Never Dubai is a very bad place

JAMIE Come on it can't be that bad

TAXI DRIVER Maybe you don't know Dubai

JAMIE Tell me why it's a bad place?

TAXI DRIVER If an Emirati comes in my taxi for a long journey and after refuses to pay me and I go to the police – they laugh at me

If anyone makes complaint against me I pay 1000-dirham fine even if it not my fault

If I complain they laugh at me

Almost every week two weeks this happen

I don't make money. I lose money

If I complain to the company. They laugh at me

Here I am not human

JAMIE There must be someone you can complain to?

TAXI DRIVER My friend, my friend drove two Emirati men to the desert

When they arrive they don't want to pay

He got angry. Maybe he shouted

They found him in the desert, in his taxi, they hung him with his tie

They left him in the desert for one week

Now you see I am not wearing a tie. They changed the
uniform because the drivers was scared, we are scared to
wear a tie

JAMIE I'm sorry

TAXI DRIVER Why are you sorry?

JAMIE I don't know, it's an expression

TAXI DRIVER British people say sorry all the time, why?

A pause.

JAMIE Maybe we feel guilty

TAXI DRIVER Maybe that's why your people cry

Scene 9

Eighty-eighth floor of Vision tTowers. **AMAR** *is standing on the edge of the roof. A* **CAMP OFFICIAL** *appears.*

AMAR I would work better, work harder

CAMP OFFICIAL If

AMAR If I was in better accommodation

CAMP OFFICIAL Would you?

AMAR Of course. I would rest more, exercise on the cricket field, I would / be

CAMP OFFICIAL More productive

AMAR Exactly

CAMP OFFICIAL You could wake up early in the morning and have chamomile tea in an empty cricket field and watch the / sunrise

AMAR I could cook my mother's recipes in the / kitchen

CAMP OFFICIAL You could watch TV while slouching on a beanbag

AMAR I could have hot / showers

CAMP OFFICIAL Isn't this camp good enough for you?

AMAR Shouldn't we always want more?

CAMP OFFICIAL Yes

AMAR Better?

CAMP OFFICIAL Yes

AMAR Bigger?

CAMP OFFICIAL Do you think you're special?

AMAR I work hard

CAMP OFFICIAL Everybody works hard

AMAR I have a young daughter

CAMP OFFICIAL Everyone has daughters

AMAR I'm far away from home

CAMP OFFICIAL We're all strangers here

AMAR I can pay

CAMP OFFICIAL You're already in debt

> *Beat.*

AMAR I have information

CAMP OFFICIAL What kind?

AMAR The good kind
But

CAMP OFFICIAL But?

AMAR I want your word

CAMP OFFICIAL My word

AMAR That you'll get me to the other camp

CAMP OFFICIAL Depends on the information

> AMAR *looks around. He approaches the* CAMP OFFICIAL *and whispers in his ear.*

I need more

AMAR More? I don't have more

CAMP OFFICIAL Who told you?

AMAR Someone

CAMP OFFICIAL Name?

AMAR I don't know

CAMP OFFICIAL You don't know?

AMAR No. I don't know

CAMP OFFICIAL So a stranger told you?

AMAR We're all strangers here

CAMP OFFICIAL Someone you've never seen before just walked up to you / and

AMAR Exactly

The CAMP OFFICIAL *thinks it over.*

CAMP OFFICIAL Then it's not enough

Beat.

AMAR If I told you, what would you do / with –

CAMP OFFICIAL The information?

AMAR Yes what would you do with – the information?

CAMP OFFICIAL We'll process it

AMAR And?

CAMP OFFICIAL And act accordingly

AMAR Will you do anything to the information?

CAMP OFFICIAL Depends

AMAR Will you hurt the information?

CAMP OFFICIAL Depends

AMAR On?

CAMP OFFICIAL On how the information behaves

AMAR It's very good information

CAMP OFFICIAL I'm sure he is

Beat.

AMAR He likes cricket

CAMP OFFICIAL Green

AMAR His wife is a great cook

CAMP OFFICIAL Fresh

AMAR He misses the smell of the sea

CAMP OFFICIAL Swimming pool

AMAR I think he's a father

CAMP OFFICIAL Ice cream

AMAR In the stars

CAMP OFFICIAL Shiny

AMAR Everywhere

CAMP OFFICIAL Hot

AMAR Shower

CAMP OFFICIAL Chamomile

AMAR Tea

CAMP OFFICIAL Beanbag

AMAR TV

CAMP OFFICIAL Happy

AMAR Money

CAMP OFFICIAL Friends

AMAR Stupid

CAMP OFFICIAL Life

AMAR More

CAMP OFFICIAL Bigger

AMAR Better

CAMP OFFICIAL Love

AMAR Lali

They are silent for a moment. **AMAR** *approaches the* **CAMP OFFICIAL** *and whispers in his ear again.*

Scene 10

Emirates Hills. JAMIE *and* TOMMIE *sit in a bar. It is on the 67th floor of a hotel. It is light and minimal. There is a large aquarium behind them. They are drinking whiskey.*

TOMMIE My neighbour right, goes on holiday, back to Amaan or Tehran or wherever he's from. He gets delayed on his trip for a few weeks, as you do, and he's got this car right, this nice big expensive car parked on the street outside his house

JAMIE It got nicked

TOMMIE No

JAMIE It got shat on by a falcon

TOMMIE Shut up – so while he's away there's a dust storm, so this car obviously, you know it gets dirty and dusty, it gets worse and worse as the days go by. When he gets back from his trip he finds a fine on his car for – get this - damaging the aesthetic appearance of Dubai

JAMIE That's ridiculous

TOMMIE Best way to run a country mate

JAMIE What fining people for dust negligence?

TOMMIE No making sure everyone pulls their weight, you know does their bit

JAMIE It's a bit unfair, I mean it's not his fault there was a dust storm

TOMMIE Fairness doesn't come into it Jamie. You don't build the world's tallest building, the world's largest mall and the world's largest artificial island by being fair

JAMIE There's more to a country than its landmarks

TOMMIE It's not a country Jamie – it's a business

Beat.

JAMIE How long you lived here again?

TOMMIE Almost ten years now

JAMIE That's a long time

TOMMIE Well I love it here. My wife loves it here, my kids love it here. Our life Jamie, our life is infinitely better than back home

In fact, everyone in Dubai is happy

JAMIE Well not *everyone* surely?

TOMMIE Look *(he gestures at the rest of the people in the bar)*

JAMIE It's a bar Tommie, everyone's pissed

TOMMIE Pissed but happy

Beat.

JAMIE Bumped into an old friend of mine, she's in town for work, sort of a journalist

TOMMIE Oh yeah?

JAMIE She was banging on about the construction workers, you know their working conditions and that

TOMMIE Journos love all that chat

JAMIE So I looked up some articles online, and some of the stuff that they're saying goes on here, I mean it's pretty –

TOMMIE Jamie – virtually every couple of weeks some Western journo pops over here and writes some poorly researched drivel about the "Dark side of Dubai" –

JAMIE I've gotta say though some of the stuff I read / sounded pretty damn–

TOMMIE It really pisses me off – they come here, spend a few days in the sun at a five-star beach resort, chat to a few workers, write down a few little anecdotes, and then jet off back to their comfortable middle class lives and write some sensationalist crap about expats eating 100 quid gold dipped, lobster infused sushi while gawking at workers sweating away in the sun - which as we both know is total bollocks

JAMIE Alright but surely there's got to be some truth to it somewhere

TOMMIE I'm not saying those lads don't have a hard life, the job's bloody hard graft but you gotta look at the bigger picture mate

JAMIE And what is the bigger picture?

TOMMIE South Asia, and this is fact, gets more cash from migrants sending money back home from working abroad than all foreign aid combined

JAMIE And where did you hear that?

TOMMIE It's an official figure you can look it up

Without these jobs see, you're talking about a massive rise in poverty back in their countries –

JAMIE But the conditions Tommie, it must be fucking awful. twelve hour days, six day weeks and the pay - I don't know it / just seems –

TOMMIE I saw a picture once in the Guardian or Time magazine or something like that, and it was of this young lad, Indian lad, he looked no more than fifteen, let's call him, I don't know, Sandeep right. So Sandeep works in some sort of quarry in India shifting bricks. They each weigh about forty kilos, if he shifts a hundred in a day he gets the equivalent of about four US dollars. He works in a pair of shorts, sandals, no gloves, no helmet, no facemask - nothing. On top of that he has to pay rent, transport, food - the whole lot - so he can forget about saving / any money

JAMIE What's your point?

TOMMIE The point is Jamie, if he came to Dubai his life would be significantly better, he'd get a minimum of two hundred dollars a month - if not more, half of which he's able to send back to support his family or put away. He's provided with free accommodation, meals, transport and a month's annual leave, every one or /two years

JAMIE Yeah I / guess

TOMMIE And on top of all that he's not scrambling around in toxic materials half naked wearing flipping sandals - here Sandeep gets safety gear, protective clothing, access to company healthcare - whole shebang

JAMIE If you put it that way

TOMMIE I'm not *putting* it any *way*, that's just how it is, that's the truth, the reality

JAMIE So you're saying the industry, the jobs, it's basically a lifeline for these guys

TOMMIE Exactly, they're sending money home to build houses, start small businesses

JAMIE It's pretty much lifting these people out of poverty

TOMMIE In fact the irony is that these leftie journos save-the-world types are probably doing a massive disservice to the very people they claim to be helping

JAMIE How?

TOMMIE Putting off potential investors, putting off migrants from coming over here, scaring them away

JAMIE Cutting off opportunities

TOMMIE And of course there are worse industries all over the world with worse conditions, but the thing is Dubai is an easy target because it's brash and bright and in your face

JAMIE And full of tacky expats scoffing gold dipped lobster infused sushi

TOMMIE And it's run by Arab men in white dresses

Beat.

JAMIE She wants me to help her

TOMMIE Who?

JAMIE My friend, the journalist

TOMMIE Help her how?

JAMIE She wants to chat to some workers, see where they work, where they live

TOMMIE What'd you say?

JAMIE I told her to bugger off

TOMMIE You should take her to one of the accommodation villages

JAMIE What for?

TOMMIE Prove her wrong

JAMIE How would that prove her wrong?

TOMMIE She'll see that they're not living in some squalid labour camp like she thinks

JAMIE You been?

TOMMIE Yeah

JAMIE What's it like?

TOMMIE The rooms are small but they're spotless, they've got modern fully kitted-out kitchens for them to cook in, there's free wi-fi and a Skype room to call home from, and there are these TV rooms with channels in Bengali, Urdu all their different languages, there's even a cricket field

JAMIE And it's alright to take a visitor there?

TOMMIE Sure get it cleared with Amanda – tell her it could generate good publicity, she'll be all over it

The WAITER *appears.*

WAITER Excuse me, would you like another drink?

TOMMIE I would love another drink my friend. Where you from?

WAITER India

TOMMIE Tell me is your life better here or in India?

WAITER Of course in Dubai. It is much better

TOMMIE See?

Scene 11

The 88th floor of the Vision Tower construction site in Business Bay. AMAR *stands alone.* TANVEER *appears.*

AMAR Look at all the lights, they look like stars

TANVEER Why did you do it?

AMAR When my building is finished there's going to be a fireworks display that can be seen from space

TANVEER Why did you do it?

AMAR From space!

TANVEER Why?

AMAR The more you work

TANVEER Look at me

AMAR The bigger you are

TANVEER Look at me. Look at me

AMAR The more you work the bigger you are

TANVEER I know it was you

AMAR I want to be so big that I can be seen from space

TANVEER Just tell me why? Why did you do it?

AMAR All the astronauts orbiting around the Earth, they'll look down out of their little round windows and they'll see me, standing on the top floor of Vision Towers / huge and glowing

TANVEER I'm so tired I'm so tired

AMAR *seems to notice* TANVEER *for the first time.*

AMAR It's so hot

TANVEER Balan

AMAR When?

TANVEER Today

AMAR How?

TANVEER Heart attack

AMAR How old?

TANVEER Twenty-three

AMAR It's so hot

TANVEER Pavalan

AMAR How?

TANVEER He fell

AMAR What floor?

TANVEER Fifty-fifth

AMAR I'm so tired

>   *Beat.*

TANVEER Why?

AMAR I wanted to move to the camp with the cricket field

TANVEER And the shiny floors

AMAR And the beanbags

TANVEER And the chamomile tea

AMAR And the hot showers

TANVEER It may look like I'm calm but –

AMAR But?

TANVEER In my head I've already killed you three times

AMAR The funny thing is –

TANVEER Is?

AMAR I don't even think there is a camp with a cricket field

TANVEER We're all paying the price. We're all paying the price now

AMAR I'm sorry

TANVEER I don't care

AMAR I'm sorry

TANVEER It's too late

AMAR I just / wanted

TANVEER You disgust me

AMAR I'm –

TANVEER You disgust me

Beat.

AMAR Listen

TANVEER To what?

AMAR Can you hear that?

TANVEER No

AMAR I can hear the waves of the Persian Gulf

TANVEER Stop it

AMAR It sounds like Kerala

TANVEER Stop it

AMAR It's so beautiful. Shhhh. There listen do you hear it?

TANVEER No

AMAR I can hear the waves of the Persian Gulf. And if I close my eyes. If I close my eyes, I can see your face Lali. I can see your face and it's glowing

Scene 12

JAMIE's apartment in Dubai Marina. It is on the 72nd floor. There is a large amount of glass, everything is minimal, clean and expensive. The night skyline dominates the room, it is mesmerising as it glitters and glows. CLARA stands at the largest window looking out over the Marina, she has her back to the room and to JAMIE. JAMIE is seated in the living room watching her. They are quiet for a moment.

CLARA Jesus

JAMIE What?

CLARA There's something –

JAMIE What is it?

CLARA I can't believe I'm saying this – but there's something exciting about all the buildings

JAMIE This was all scrubland a few years ago

CLARA I feel like I'm in a movie

She turns around and looks at the apartment.

This apartment is ridiculous

JAMIE Do you like it?

She surveys the apartment.

CLARA No. It's repulsive

Beat.

I'm joking. It's beautiful

I'm happy for you

JAMIE Costs a fucking fortune

CLARA I can tell

JAMIE And you have to pay rent a year up front in Dubai

CLARA How the hell do people manage that?

JAMIE They practically hand you a credit card when you get off the plane.

I've got three

CLARA Jesus

Can I have a drink?

JAMIE Sure – beer?

CLARA Cold

JAMIE exits.

CLARA walks around the room. She touches things, maybe picks something up and examines it.

JAMIE enters with a beer.

Why did you call me?

JAMIE I didn't want to leave things you know

CLARA Sour?

JAMIE Yeah

Beat.

How's the research going?

CLARA I spend my days in cafes trying to locate the most miserable looking waiters and then follow them home and try and interview them

JAMIE Are you serious?

CLARA No of course not you knob

JAMIE I wouldn't put it past you

CLARA I'll take that as a compliment

JAMIE I've been thinking about what you said

CLARA And?

JAMIE I was speaking to a colleague and well I can take you to
see one of the company's accommodation villages
If you're interested

CLARA What the hell's an accommodation village?

JAMIE It's where the workers, the construction workers live

CLARA They're called accommodation villages?

JAMIE Yeah

CLARA Who thought that one up?

JAMIE I'm offering to help you Clara

CLARA Can I film?

JAMIE No

CLARA Secretly?

JAMIE No

CLARA Can I speak to them?

JAMIE I don't know I'll find out

CLARA Accommodation village?

JAMIE They have TV rooms and Skype and chamomile tea

CLARA Sounds like a Scandinavian prison

JAMIE It's not a prison, it's an / accommodation –

CLARA Why do you suddenly want to help me?

JAMIE Well yesterday while I was driving to work I
I realised how happy I was to see you again

CLARA It's good to see you too

Beat.

Cheers

JAMIE Cheers

CLARA Maybe you're not such a dick after all

JAMIE And also Clara

Well I... I want to prove you wrong

Scene 13

An office in Media City, on the 114th floor. JAMIE *sits at his laptop, he is watching the live feed. The skyline surrounds him.*

AMAR *stands on the rooftop of the 88th floor of the construction site in Business Bay. The skyline has started to glimmer behind him.*

AMAR Look I can see the future

What's it like?

I can see the future my darling

And it's terrifying

When I looked at the buildings I used to see swimming pools on the roofs. I used to see shining glass. I used to see people eating dinner. Families watching TV and laughing. Children on the balconies eating ice cream

Now when I look at the buildings all I see is your face

And your face Lali, your face it's glowing

I'm so sorry

I'm so sorry

I let you down my darling

I let everybody down

I don't know how to come home

How do I come home?

I don't know how to come home

How do I come home?

I'm so small, look how small I am Lali, I'm too small to come home

Nobody cares

Nobody cares

I built this building

I built this building

I built this building

Can you see me my little one?

AMAR *waves.*

JAMIE *who is still looking at the screen waves back.*

Can you see me standing here in the stars?

Look at me I'm in the future

Yes the future – can you believe it?

A pigeon flies across the stage. It lands next to **AMAR.** *He picks it up and strokes it. He holds the pigeon to his chest and walks off the edge of the eighty-eighth floor.*

Scene 14

Moments after AMAR *has jumped.* JAMIE *is still sitting at his laptop.*

JAMIE Tommie, Tommie

Oh God, oh Jesus, shit

TOMMIE *enters.*

TOMMIE What is it?

JAMIE Someone just jumped

TOMMIE What do you mean jumped – like up and down?

JAMIE No like jumped off – someone just jumped off the top, right off the top of the construction site, it must be like the 80th floor Jesus

TOMMIE Oh shit

JAMIE Tommie

TOMMIE What mate?

JAMIE Do you think he's alright?

TOMMIE No I don't think he's alright Jamie

JAMIE He was waving

TOMMIE What?

JAMIE He was waving

TOMMIE What you talking about?

JAMIE I thought he might be waving at me, just before he...

He was standing near the edge, sort of just staring out and then he waved and then he was holding something, stroking it, then he just walked off – he didn't jump, he didn't fall or anything – he just sort of kept walking straight off the edge

Beat.

TOMMIE It was probably an accident, don't worry about it mate, these things happen, it's / a construction site

JAMIE It wasn't an accident, it can't have been. Who do you think he was waving at? Do you think he was waving at me?

TOMMIE I don't know Jamie. Jesus what a fucking mess

JAMIE What do we do?

TOMMIE I better call / Amanda

JAMIE Call an ambulance

TOMMIE He's dead Jamie. He's in pieces on the pavement. It's the eighty-eighth floor

JAMIE We should find out why he did it

TOMMIE What does it matter why he did it Jamie?

JAMIE Well so we can stop it happening again. You know prevention / damage limitation

TOMMIE We can't let this get out. For starters delete that bloody footage

JAMIE They might need it for the investigation

TOMMIE There isn't going to be an investigation

Delete it

JAMIE Yeah of course

TOMMIE I'm gonna go and tell Amanda

JAMIE He just walked off

TOMMIE Jamie?

JAMIE Yes?

TOMMIE Are you alright?

JAMIE Yeah I'm fine

JAMIE sits down. He watches the video again. He gets up to leave. He hesistates at the door. Walks back to the computer. He takes out a USB and makes a copy of the footage.

Scene 15

TOMMIE, DEENA and JAMIE are sitting in a hotel restaurant. It's an all-day brunch, electronic music pumps in the background. Empty bottles fill the table. Everyone has already had a little bit too much to drink. A WAITER stands motionless in the background throughout the scene. A portrait of Sheikh Mohammed bin Rashid Al Maktoum hangs in the background.

TOMMIE This might be a bit controversial

But if you think about it

He sort of – inaugurated the building

DEENA You're right

We should have had a ribbon at the edge for him to cut as he walked off

TOMMIE We could have read out a ceremonial poem, with rhyming couplets

He clears his throat.

The following is delivered in a mock Indian accent.

Dubai

A slight pause.

Goodbye

DEENA *laughs.* JAMIE *does not.*

Do you not like the poem Jamie?

JAMIE It's a bit insensitive

TOMMIE Oh come on we're just having a bit of a laugh, right Deena?

DEENA Cheer up Jamie it's not like anybody died

Oh wait

TOMMIE *and* **DEENA** *exchange looks and laugh.*

JAMIE A man – one of our employees just killed himself. Have a bit of respect

DEENA I'm sorry Jamie

TOMMIE Me too

Beat.

Dubai

DEENA Goodbye

JAMIE Really?

TOMMIE Come on mate people in London are always throwing themselves in front of the tube

And I know exactly what you think when you're sitting there on the Piccadilly line, rush hour, on your way to a zone five flat full of strangers, some smelly fat bloke leaning into you, your little Marks and Sparks ready meal clutched in your sweaty hands and the announcement comes through that there's "a person under the train" and you're stuck in a tunnel for I don't know how long and you think – bloody selfish bugger couldn't he have just hung himself at home?

JAMIE This is different

DEENA How?

JAMIE It just is

You know it is

I'm surprised at you Deena

DEENA Why?

JAMIE Because –

DEENA Because I'm a woman?

TOMMIE Sexist

JAMIE No because you're Indian

DEENA What because I'm brown I should feel more

TOMMIE Stop being a racist Jamie

DEENA Yeah stop being a racist

    JAMIE *and* DEENA *laugh.*

JAMIE I'm not being racist, I just thought you might show some more concern for your fellow citizens

DEENA It's not my fault the guy was depressed. What do you want me to do about it? Start an Indian counselling group?

JAMIE Someone has to take some sort of responsibility

DEENA Who me?

JAMIE No I mean the government should do something

TOMMIE What government?

JAMIE This government, and the Indian government too – they should investigate these things

TOMMIE It's a suicide, what is there to investigate?

JAMIE Well if it's linked

TOMMIE Linked to what?

JAMIE The job, financial pressure, I don't know

TOMMIE Even if it is, it's hardly an epidemic

DEENA And anyway this guy could have topped himself here or back home, we'll never know why he did it

JAMIE I guess but there's no need to be so cruel about the guy

DEENA Relax it's just a bit of comic relief

Beat.

TOMMIE Do you need some counselling Jamie?

JAMIE Shut up

DEENA It's nothing to be ashamed of

TOMMIE She's right there's nothing to be ashamed of

JAMIE No I don't need any counselling just cut it out

CLARA *enters, she looks around for* JAMIE.

TOMMIE Is that who you're waiting for?

JAMIE Who?

TOMMIE Your girlfriend?

JAMIE She's not my girlfriend
    Clara

CLARA *spots* JAMIE *and walks over.*

CLARA This is...nice

JAMIE Tommie, Deena this is Clara

CLARA Hello

DEENA Hello Clara

TOMMIE Drink?

CLARA Yes please

TOMMIE *signals to the* WAITER *who comes over and silently fills a glass of champagne for* CLARA.

DEENA Jamie said you're a shopping journalist

CLARA Well Jamie's wrong

DEENA You're not a shopping correspondent?

CLARA Sorry to disappoint

TOMMIE So if you're not a shopping correspondent, what do you do?

CLARA I'm a journalist

DEENA Why are you here?

CLARA To get pissed apparently

DEENA No I mean in Dubai

CLARA Oh sorry. Well... I'm investigating conditions, working conditions

DEENA What kind of working conditions?

CLARA Construction workers / actually

JAMIE Clara not now / come on

DEENA Well that's funny

CLARA Is it?

DEENA We were just chatting about this guy, this worker who jumped off one of the / building sites today

TOMMIE I wouldn't go blabbing to a journalist about / that Deena

CLARA When did this happen?

DEENA Today

CLARA He killed himself?

DEENA Pretty / much

TOMMIE You've got such a big gob / Deena

DEENA What? There's nothing to hide, the man was sad or angry or I don't know what and he jumped off the eighty-eighth floor

CLARA Does anyone know why he did it?

DEENA Could be anything really

CLARA Do you know his name?

JAMIE No we don't, let's / move on

DEENA She's only asking a few / bloody questions

JAMIE So what's the entertainment today?

TOMMIE Karaoke

DEENA I love Karaoke! Jamie let's do a song

JAMIE No way

CLARA He's actually a great singer

JAMIE I'm not

DEENA Come on Jamie let's go and put our names down

JAMIE No

DEENA You're so mean, just one song

JAMIE No

DEENA But Clara said you were a great singer

JAMIE I'm not

CLARA Don't be a bore Jamie, do a bloody song

DEENA Yeah Jamie you've already been sexist and racist today don't be boring as / well

JAMIE Alright, come on then

> JAMIE *and* DEENA *exit.*

Beat.

TOMMIE Enjoying your trip?

CLARA Well I wouldn't use the word *enjoy*

TOMMIE Not lived up to your expectations?

CLARA It's a work trip I'm pretty busy with research

TOMMIE Is this research?

CLARA Well everybody needs a night off

Beat.

TOMMIE So what exactly are you researching then?

CLARA I'm trying to find evidence of violations

TOMMIE Safety violations?

CLARA That sort of thing

TOMMIE It's all pretty up to standard round here

CLARA Well actually it's more human rights violations I'm interested in

TOMMIE Oh yeah, like what?

CLARA Well, where to begin? Confiscation of passports, violation of maximum working hours, withholding of wages, inadequate living conditions / bonded labour

TOMMIE Bloody hell heavy stuff

Beat.

Do you have a lot of evidence then?

CLARA Well there are already a lot of witness accounts out there

TOMMIE Anecdotal

CLARA First-hand accounts from the workers collected by other journalists human rights activists, people like that

TOMMIE So your information and opinions are based on *my mate told me* kind of anecdotes

CLARA I wouldn't put it like that no

TOMMIE What's it based on then?

CLARA People's research

TOMMIE Not your own

CLARA At the moment no

TOMMIE So at the moment it's hearsay / conjecture

CLARA It's not hearsay

TOMMIE I know your type, there's always a couple of journos in town doing a bit of Dubai bashing

CLARA I'm not here to do any bashing

TOMMIE A bit of first-world condescension and finger wagging for the Emiratis then?

CLARA Jesus you're a bit full on

TOMMIE I'm just trying to have some good chat

CLARA Sure of course

Beat.

I guess we're sort of coming from different angles

TOMMIE The difference between people like me and people like you Clara is that you've got this big chip on your shoulder about being white and European and privileged and that's the reason you hate Dubai

CLARA I don't hate Dubai, I just don't agree with certain / employment practices –

TOMMIE You hate Dubai because the very flaws you want to expose are exactly the same as ours back home, it's just that here you can claim you're not complicit in the system, but back in the UK you / can't do that

CLARA I'm not complicit in any system

TOMMIE In case you haven't noticed the UK takes advantage of cheap labour all over the bloody world and you – you take part in that every day, every time you buy a coffee or a / pair of bloody tights

CLARA Yeah well I try my / best to avoid –

TOMMIE And on top of that you've formed your opinion of Dubai based on factually inaccurate, poorly researched, anecdotal / evidence

CLARA *You* sound like the one with a chip on / his shoulder

TOMMIE And just look at the UK's bloody history when it comes to outsourcing labour –

CLARA Well that's not my fault is it? And / anyway –

TOMMIE My point is Clara that as a resident of the UK you don't have the moral high ground to criticise and bash the inequality of any other country's society or economic / policy

CLARA So you're saying we don't have a responsibility to call out major human rights violations / just because

TOMMIE Not when you're excluding significant details because they don't fit into your little humanitarian narrative –

CLARA Like what?

TOMMIE Like the huge financial benefits these jobs have for the labourers, it's a way out of poverty that their own governments can't / ever provide

CLARA But the conditions are inhumane

TOMMIE Well they're better than what they could ever experience back home

CLARA It's illogical to suggest that a given situation is acceptable simply because it could be worse off

TOMMIE So you'd rather they live in shanty towns earning less than half the money they / earn here

CLARA No of course I wouldn't rather that, I –

DEENA *and* JAMIE *enter.*

DEENA Guess what?

CLARA What?

DEENA We're going to sing *I Believe I Can Fly* – how fucking hilarious is that?

Scene 16

JAMIE's flat. The next morning. He sits in his living room, his laptop is open. The skyline looms large behind him. It feels more menacing than before.

The doorbell rings. He opens the door. CLARA *walks in. He looks at her in confusion for a moment, before realising why she is there.*

JAMIE Shit I'm sorry

CLARA I waited for over an hour

I called you a million times

JAMIE I'm sorry, I had too much to drink last night and I –

CLARA Forgot

JAMIE It completely slipped my mind about the –

CLARA Accommodation village

JAMIE And my phone / was

CLARA On silent

JAMIE Come in

CLARA By the way that Tommie guy is a right ranting dick

JAMIE Give it a rest Clara

Beat.

CLARA I got into a labour camp last night

JAMIE When?

CLARA After the piss-up brunch thing

JAMIE How the / hell –

CLARA I rented a car and I waited outside a huge construction site somewhere near Internet City

When the shift finished, I followed the bus back to the camp
And I just drove in, in between two buses

JAMIE What was it like?

CLARA There's no chamomile tea Jamie if that's what you're asking

JAMIE That's not what I'm asking

CLARA It's like a big black hole

There're no street lights. It looks like a derelict factory

And the smell

There's an overwhelming smell of shit, but not just any shit, it stinks of actual human shit

JAMIE Did you speak to anyone?

CLARA No I got found out pretty quickly

JAMIE Did you film anything?

CLARA I did but they took it off me

JAMIE Who did?

CLARA The camp boss or guard whatever he is

He found me, asked me to leave, searched my bag and took my camera

JAMIE Maybe they're not all like that, the camps

CLARA You keep telling yourself that

Beat.

You know the guy

JAMIE Guy? What guy?

CLARA The guy who you know

JAMIE No I don't know

CLARA The guy who jumped

JAMIE What about him?

CLARA What do you know about him?

JAMIE I don't know anything

CLARA Can you find out something, anything?

JAMIE I thought that was your job? You're the journalist

CLARA Can you at least find out his name?

Just his name

Beat.

JAMIE I saw him

CLARA You saw him?

JAMIE Yeah

CLARA What do you mean you saw him?

JAMIE I saw him, you know

CLARA You mean?

JAMIE Yeah, jump. I saw him jump

CLARA What? What do you mean you saw him jump? How?

JAMIE We have this live feed thing set up, live footage –

CLARA You saw it on video?

JAMIE He sort of just walked off

eighty-eighth floor

He hesitates.

I have it

It's on film

CLARA What you have it here?

JAMIE Yeah

CLARA Are you serious?

JAMIE Yes

CLARA Can I see it?

Beat.

JAMIE No

CLARA Why not?

JAMIE Because it's disturbing, it's someone's death for Christ's sake

CLARA Jamie let me see it

JAMIE Look I don't even know why I told you I shouldn't have / said anything-

CLARA Well you can't tell me about it and then not show me, let me see it

JAMIE No

CLARA Oh come on

JAMIE *considers it.*

JAMIE No, look this is weird / it's -

CLARA It's just a video Jamie please

JAMIE No

CLARA Come on just a quick look

JAMIE God you're annoying. Fine. Here watch it

JAMIE *plays the film on his laptop. They watch in silence. A moment passes.*

CLARA Can I have a copy?

JAMIE Are you joking?

CLARA No I'm serious

JAMIE Of course you can't, are you mental? I'd lose my job

CLARA Jamie you need to give me a copy

JAMIE I don't need to do anything

CLARA Why did you show it to me then?

Why did you even make a copy?

JAMIE I don't know... I needed to tell / someone

CLARA Jamie / listen

JAMIE ...and you were being so bloody pushy

CLARA Listen, if you give me / a copy -

JAMIE You don't seriously think I'm actually going to even think about giving you a copy?

CLARA This is really important

JAMIE I don't care how important it is

CLARA Jamie

JAMIE I can't give you a copy Clara. This is a / ridiculous conversation-

CLARA Jamie just imagine it, his family, shattered broken waiting in the arrival hall at the airport for a fucking coffin, he's probably got kids / imagine

JAMIE Clara please just / leave it –

CLARA Imagine his kid, his little kid still hoping, thinking that maybe just somehow, the tiniest little hope burrowed deep down in her heart, that just maybe her daddy will walk out of those doors just like he promised, and all she gets is a fucking pine box with his name scribbled on the side

And then - guess who is at departures - who's at departures Jamie?

JAMIE I don't know. Who?

CLARA A new batch of them – a new group of hopefuls, queuing up with their passports clutched in their nervous sweaty hands, off to build a better life for themselves, for their families but little do they know eh?

Why don't you care Jamie?

You used to care so much, don't you remember?

JAMIE Oh Sorry, forgive me for not wanting to throw away my own job in aid of your big career break

CLARA This is so much bigger than all that

JAMIE Oh is it now?

CLARA Yeah it is. People's lives are being wasted and lost so you can have all this..this..this shit and so you can get pissed and draw cocks all over the place for a laugh

JAMIE It's that simple is it?

CLARA Yeah it is actually

JAMIE So what this sofa, some poor worker somewhere died so I could own this sofa?

CLARA Oh don't be so thick

JAMIE Don't be so self-righteous

CLARA Do you know what your problem is?

JAMIE No. Please enlighten me

CLARA You've got no integrity

No backbone

JAMIE And so what? So fucking what?

CLARA What's wrong with you?

JAMIE Quite a bit apparently

CLARA Why don't you care even a tiny little bit?

JAMIE Because I want to be rich

I was always fighting against it, like it was a dirty secret or something

And now I've got it Clara, I can have whatever I want

Anything, anything I want

And it feels so good. It's so pleasurable

You don't understand the level of pleasure

I don't have to worry about anything

I don't have to care about anything

I don't even have to pretend I / care

CLARA But it's not real, none of this is / real

JAMIE I didn't come to Dubai for anything real

I've already lived in real places and they're shit, they're horrible

And anyway, it won't make a difference, it's not going to change anything, no one cares Clara, no one gives a shit, it's just a video, in a week it will be totally insignificant

CLARA That's not true, this is how change starts, this is/how things

JAMIE Open your eyes Clara, you're not gonna change the world. Go and harass someone else with your bleeding heart and your humanity and beg them for your big break

A pause.

CLARA I shouldn't have asked I'm sorry

I'm sorry

I got carried away it wasn't right

Look let's just forget you showed me the video alright?

Alright?

JAMIE Alright

CLARA I shouldn't have asked and I won't bring it up again

I promise

JAMIE Good

CLARA I'm sorry / I'm sorry

JAMIE It's fine

CLARA It was really inappropriate for me to ask you to / give me

JAMIE I said it's fine. Let's move on

Do you want a coffee?

CLARA Yeah

JAMIE *gets up and heads towards the kitchen.*

JAMIE *looks at* CLARA, *he looks over at his laptop, the USB with the footage plugged into it. He hesitates, he looks at* CLARA *again and then turns around and walks to the kitchen.*

CLARA *walks over to the laptop, she takes out a USB from her bag, as quickly as she can, she puts it into* JAMIE*'s laptop and copies the footage. She keeps one eye on the kitchen door. She gets what she needs and puts her USB back in the bag, seconds before* JAMIE *enters again with coffee.*

CLARA Is this fairtrade?

JAMIE Fuck off

CLARA It's a joke. I was completely joking, I swear!

JAMIE *looks at her and then laughs*

JAMIE I'll give it to you, that wasn't bad

Scene 17

LALI, AMAR'*s daughter, 11 years old, Indian, is waiting at the arrivals hall at an airport in Kerala, she is holding a bunch of flowers.*

ANNOUNCER Flight 952 from Dubai has just landed

Flight 952 from Dubai has landed

Flight 952 from Dubai has landed

Scene 18

AMANDA *and* JAMIE *are watching the live feed from the construction site. The live feed can be seen by the audience. It is projected into the space and fills the stage from all angles. As the scene goes on, the footage gradually speeds up, until it reaches a dizzying speed.*

AMANDA It's sort of mesmerising isn't it?

JAMIE I know what you mean

AMANDA I think it's symbolic

JAMIE Symbolic?

AMANDA Yes you see these men they're not just building the physical building but they're also in a sort of metaphorical way building their own futures

They're building their way out of poverty

JAMIE I wonder if the clients, I wonder what they see when they look at them

AMANDA Oh they only see equity, money, investment

JAMIE Maybe we could make them see beyond that

AMANDA You're full of optimism aren't you Jamie?

JAMIE Shouldn't I be?

AMANDA No it's wonderful, it's refreshing, you're a real go-getter aren't you?

JAMIE Yeah I guess you could say that

Beat.

AMANDA Good weekend?

JAMIE Great

AMANDA I went to the desert

JAMIE Oh yeah was it good?

AMANDA It's very beautiful

JAMIE It is yeah

AMANDA I was standing there, in the desert, and suddenly Jamie I had this urge, this longing to go back to when there was an infinite nothingness

JAMIE Got to love the desert

AMANDA Have you ever felt that Jamie?

JAMIE No not specifically

AMANDA Have you ever been to the desert?

JAMIE I have yes

AMANDA What did you think?

JAMIE It was very big and
    sandy

AMANDA Take a seat Jamie

JAMIE Cheers

    Beat.

AMANDA Do you feel sorry for them? *(She gestures to the live feed)*

JAMIE For the workers?

AMANDA Do you pity them?

JAMIE Erm...yeah a bit I guess yeah, I mean I have much more than they do so...

AMANDA Is that why you did it?

JAMIE Did what?

AMANDA Don't play the fool Jamie, it's embarrassing

JAMIE I'm not playing anything I swear, I don't know what you're referring to

AMANDA Someone released the footage Jamie

JAMIE What footage?

AMANDA Of that poor man's suicide. I woke up this morning and suddenly it's everywhere, it's all over the internet, and the news, they've tracked down his family, human rights activists are sharpening their spears as we speak, they're claiming it's a sign of exploitation

JAMIE Shit

AMANDA Yes it is shit isn't it? And I have this tiny little hunch that just maybe possibly it was you

JAMIE What?

AMANDA What? What do you mean *what?* What kind of idiotic response is that? What? What?

You're a child Jamie

You can't handle the world

JAMIE Amanda of course it wasn't me, why would I do / that?

AMANDA I don't know Jamie. Why would / you?

JAMIE Amanda I didn't release / anything I swear

AMANDA Did you do it out of moral outrage, is that it? That these people are earning so little yet working so hard, and it makes you feel rotten and guilty

JAMIE Is this because I said I felt sorry for them before? Because actually I don't. I really don't. In fact I / couldn't care less

AMANDA You think that you're helping them is that it? You think you're revealing some sort of scandal?

JAMIE No of course not because I didn't release the footage

AMANDA Because there isn't a scandal, we don't even know
why the poor man did it, there could be a hundred different
reasons. And anyway these workers and their families back
home Jamie are desperately dependant on these jobs

JAMIE I know they are

AMANDA These kinds of employment programmes are actually
the most effective way to alleviate, even eliminate global
poverty

JAMIE I completely / agree

AMANDA The world as we know it is based on the fact that
somewhere far away somebody is prepared to work very hard
for very little and if you can't live with that then you should
start by chucking away your laptop, your smartphone, your
car, your flat-pack furniture, the bloody clothes on your back
and go and live in a sodding cave. A bit of whistleblowing
doesn't mean you're not / complicit any more –

JAMIE Amanda / listen

AMANDA What?

JAMIE I didn't do it, you have to/believe me

AMANDA I started with nothing. I worked my way up from the
bottom of the pile Jamie. I've worked tirelessly all my life,
I've barely had time to enjoy watching my kids grow up, or
nurse my parents in their old age, and now I'm here after
years of toil, living in cramped flats, working minimum
wage jobs, working endless evenings and weekends, and
now that I've somehow dug myself out of that hole, now my
neck is on the line because you think that you're morally
superior to an entire nation, to an entire global economy,
and the most hilarious thing is that you don't want to give
up even a single comfort from your own life

JAMIE There's been a huge misunderstanding here

AMANDA The hypocrisy is mind-blowing Jamie it / really is

JAMIE What kind of evidence have you even got?

AMANDA Tommie saw you taking the footage, he's signed a witness statement

JAMIE Jesus Christ

AMANDA If you think that all this is morally repugnant you can get off your moral high horse and fuck off back to your fucking admin job, half your wages sucked up by sodding taxes and living in a terrace in Seven fucking Sisters with six strangers, watching Polish people trudging miserably back and forth to their jobs, and under-privileged kids stuffing their fat gobs with chicken and chips and dirty kebabs and homeless people in the doorways of betting shops with their big hopeless eyes and matted beards and flea-ridden dogs and when you walk down the streets in London early in the morning, on your way to the office and everywhere, there's piles of vomit all over the pavement – everywhere bluegh bluegh bluegh – its fucking disgraceful, it's disgusting

That's what the world looks like without order, that's what happens when it's a massive free-for-all

But not here Jamie not here – here the pavements are perfect, they're spotless, in fact they employ people to scrape chewing gum off the floors of the malls – now that's progress

Dubai is an oasis of Middle Eastern progress and moderation in a land full of horror and barbarity, Dubains are building a future based on business not guns, globally competitive companies not terror networks, it creates stability and order in a region whose conflicts are spilling into our own streets, into our own streets back home Jamie. This is the future, this is the best way forward, how can you people not see that?

The reason people love Dubai – it's just no one wants to admit it – is that everybody is in their right place. Everyone knows their place

And you're going to be put in your place Jamie

It's done. It's finished. It's over

Scene 19

An interrogation room at Dubai airport. It is light and airy. There are beautiful pictures of Dubai on the walls. There are fresh flowers in vases and bowls of shiny wrapped chocolates and sweets. JAMIE *sits opposite a* GOVERNMENT OFFICIAL. *The* GOVERNMENT OFFICIAL *is calm, almost nonchalant throughout the scene.*

OFFICIAL We have a big problem

JAMIE How big?

OFFICIAL Very big

JAMIE Well what is it?

OFFICIAL We are confiscating your passport

JAMIE You can't do that

OFFICIAL We already have *(he gestures across the empty table)* look no passport

JAMIE Why what have I done?

OFFICIAL You defaulted on your debts

JAMIE I lost my job, that's what happens

I'll start paying again as soon as I find a new job in the UK

OFFICIAL It's illegal to leave the country if you are in arrears on repayments Mr

JAMIE Jamie

OFFICIAL Mr. Jamie

JAMIE You can't just take my passport, I have rights

OFFICIAL It is illegal to leave the country if you are in arrears on repayments Mr. Jamie

If you pay back the amount in full, you can have your passport

JAMIE There's no way I can get that kind of money

OFFICIAL Then we keep your passport until you get that kind of money

It's all very simple

JAMIE Are you going to arrest me?

OFFICIAL No no nothing like that

You are free to leave, go home, if you still have one, or maybe to the home of a friend, have a shower, maybe go out for dinner, have a walk on the beach, it's very beautiful at night

JAMIE I want to speak to a lawyer – to the British Embassy

OFFICIAL Go and call them as many times as you like, maybe call a friend or maybe your family. And when you have the money that you owe to the bank you can come back and take your passport

JAMIE I don't have anywhere to go

OFFICIAL You look very pale Mr. Jamie

Would you like a chocolate?

JAMIE Chocolate?

OFFICIAL Yes please help yourself

JAMIE *takes a chocolate, he unwraps it slowly, he puts it in his mouth and starts to chew, after a few bites he spits it out into his hands.*

What's the problem? You don't like marzipan?

Scene 20

A small village in Kerala, India. Four years earlier. Although poor, it is warm and colourful. It is the evening, only moments after the stars have come out in the sky. The sky is wide and full of lights. A handmade sign hangs in the background, it reads "GOODBYE DADDY". AMAR *sits outside with his daughter* LALI, *she is seven years old. They are looking out across the horizon at the sky.*

LALI They're stars

AMAR No they're not

LALI Yes they are – they're stars Dad!

AMAR They're not

LALI You're lying

AMAR Come here

Come on

Now look closely

LALI I'm looking, they're stars! You're so silly!

AMAR Try harder. Look really hard – you see they're buildings, hundreds and hundreds of sparkly buildings, the tallest buildings in the whole world – and the stars, well those are actually the lights of a thousand offices and beautiful apartments, with flat screen TVs and marble floors and swimming pools on the roofs

LALI On the roofs?

AMAR Yes on the roofs – can you see? And the restaurants, each restaurant has 200 different flavours of ice cream

LALI 200!

AMAR Yes and when you walk in the streets at night there are so many lights from all the tall buildings that it feels like you are floating in the stars in the sky

LALI How do you know Daddy?

AMAR Because I know!

LALI Who told you?

AMAR Important people who have been there – and guess what?

LALI What?

AMAR They gave me a job

LALI What kind of job?

AMAR I'm going to work in the stars and build huge buildings, so tall that they touch the clouds

LALI You're going there?

AMAR Yes

LALI *looks harder and tries to see the buildings.*

LALI Dad I can see I can see the buildings! Look

AMAR You see – I told you

LALI It's so pretty – you're going to work there?

AMAR Yes and I'm going to try all the 200 flavours of ice cream, every single one

LALI Oh that's not fair what about me?

AMAR Well, your daddy's going to work very very hard and make lots of money and then one day I'll send you a plane ticket and you can come to the stars and see me

LALI And eat ice cream

AMAR Yes we'll eat ice cream in the stars

LALI Ice cream in the stars!

AMAR And when I come back I'm going to buy a beautiful shop for you, mummy and me

A silence.

LALI Daddy?

AMAR What my darling?

LALI I'm going to miss you

AMAR Only a little bit

LALI No a big bit

AMAR Well, every time you miss me. You come here and you look out there and if you look really really really really hard - then you'll see me, standing in the stars on top of the highest building in the world

LALI But how will I know it's you? You'll be so small

AMAR I'll wave to you

LALI And I'll wave back

AMAR Exactly
And do you know what I'll be building in that city, the city in the stars?

LALI What?

AMAR I'll be building the future

LALI The future?

AMAR Yes - you see that city, that city is the city of the future
I'll be building your future

LALI Wow the future - look it's beautiful isn't it Daddy?

AMAR Very beautiful

A pause.

LALI I love you Daddy

AMAR I love you too

A pause.

LALI What is it called? The city in the stars does it have a name?

AMAR Dubailand

LALI Dubailand

Blackout.

PROPERTY LIST

Open suitcase (p2)
Chocolate bar (p2)
Evening meal (p5)
Evening meal (p5)
Picture of Dubai's ruler Sheikh Mohammed bin Rashid Al Maktoum hangs on the wall (p9)
Notebook and pen (p22)
Whiskey (p44)
Beer (p54)
Laptop (p57)
A pigeon flies across the stage (p58)
USB (p61)
Empty bottles fill the table (p62)
A portrait of Sheikh Mohammed bin Rashid Al Maktoum hangs in the background (p62)
Glass of champagne (p65)
Laptop (p71)
USB (p78)
Coffee (p78)
Bunch of flowers (p79)
There are beautiful pictures of Dubai on the walls. There are fresh flowers in vases and bowls of shiny wrapped chocolates and sweets (p85)
A handmade sign hangs in the background, it reads 'Goodbye Daddy' (p87)

Costume:
Amar – work clothes; blue overalls and safety helmet (p1)
Tommie – suit and is well groomed (p9)
Taxi Driver – uniform; a white shirt, waistcoat and black trousers (p36)

LIGHTING LIST

Dusk (p1)
He is surrounded by lights which sometimes look like stars (p1)
The glimmering skyline is tiny in the distance (p5)
Multi-coloured lights of the skyline (p32)
The lights of the skyscrapers rise and fall colouring the car's interior (p36)
The night skyline dominates the room, it is mesmerising as it

glitters and glows (p53)
The skyline has started to glimmer behind him (p57)
It is the evening, only moments after the stars have come out in the sky. The sky is wide and full of lights (p87)
Blackout (p90)

SOUND/EFFECTS LIST

A flight announcement is heard in the background during the next few lines in English, German and Arabic (p3)
Another flight announcement is heard in the background (p4)
One hundred violin strings start to play softly (9)
We hear the sound of cellos joining the violins (p9)
A soft beat joins the violins and the cellos (p10)
Voiceover: Own the lifestyle of a lifetime (p10)
The beat picks up (p10)
Voiceover: Invest in list, Invest in choice, Invest in you (p10)
An Enya style singing is added to the music, the beat quickens (p10)
Voiceover: Welcome to Dubai. Welcome to the skyline of your dreams (P10)
The music heard previously starts to play (p13)
Voiceover: Welcome to Dubai. Welcome to the future (p13)
Large birds fly overhead (p32)
He is watching the live feed (p57)
Electronic music pumps in the background (p62)
The doorbell rings (p71)
Jamie plays the film on his laptop (p74)
Amanda and Jamie are watching the life feed from the construction site. The live feed can be seen by the audience. It is projected into the space and fills the stage form all angles. As the scene goes on, the footage gradually speeds up, until it reaches a dizzying speed. (p80)

THIS IS NOT THE END